John Russel

Correspondence respecting the Alabama

John Russel

Correspondence respecting the Alabama

ISBN/EAN: 9783337728519

Printed in Europe, USA, Canada, Australia, Japan

Cover: Foto ©ninafisch / pixelio.de

More available books at **www.hansebooks.com**

NORTH AMERICA.

No. 1. (1864.)

CORRESPONDENCE

THE "ALABAMA."

(In continuation of Correspondence presented to Parliament in
March 1863.)

Presented to both Houses of Parliament by Command of Her Majesty.
1864.

LONDON:
PRINTED BY HARRISON AND SONS.

LIST OF PAPERS.

Correspondence respecting the "Alabama."

No. 1.

Mr. Adams to Earl Russell.—(Received February 21.)

My Lord,   *Legation of the United States, London, February* 19, 1863.

AT the request of my Government, I have the honour to submit to your Lordship's consideration a copy of a Memorial addressed to the Secretary of State by an Association of Underwriters in New York.

Renewing, &c.
(Signed)   CHARLES FRANCIS ADAMS.

Inclosure in No. 1.

Memorial.

YOUR Memorialists, representing the New York Mutual Insurance Company of the City of New York, respectively submit to the Department of State of the United States, the following facts, viz. :—

That the said New York Mutual Insurance Company had certain policies of insurance upon the following vessels :—Ship " Brilliant," 9,245 dollars ; ship " Manchester," 7,500 dollars ; and the said vessels, in the prosecution of their lawful voyages, were arrested on the high seas by a steamer called the " Alabama," and by her boarded and burned, and the New York Mutual Insurance Company have paid the policies of insurance on the above-named vessels in consequence of said destruction ; and your Memorialists are of opinion that the said steamer having been built at, fitted out, and sailed from a port in Great Britain, and her crew being composed principally of the subjects of the Government of Great Britain, she is to all intents and purposes a British vessel.

And your Memorialists therefore claim from the Government of Great Britain the repayment to them of the above amounts, with interest accruing thereon, and respectfully request the United States' Government to make the necessary claim on their behalf.

(Signed)   JOHN H. EARLE, *President.*
(Signed)   W. P. HANSFORD, *Secretary.*
New York, January 31, 1863.

No. 2.

Earl Russell to Mr. Adams.

Sir,   *Foreign Office, March* 9, 1863.

I HAVE the honour to acquaint you that Her Majesty's Government have had under their consideration your letter of the 19th ultimo, inclosing a copy of a Memorial which has been addressed to the United States' Secretary of State by the New York Mutual Insurance Company, claiming the repayment by Her Majesty's Government of certain policies of insurance upon the United States' vessels " Brilliant" and " Manchester," which have been destroyed on the high seas by the Confederate steam-vessel " Alabama."

I have now the honour to state to you that Her Majesty's Government entirely disclaim all responsibility for any acts of the " Alabama," and they had hoped that they had already made this decision on their part plain to the Government of the United States.

I am, &c.

(Signed) RUSSELL.

No. 3.

Earl Russell to Lord Lyons.

My Lord, Foreign Office, March 27, 1863.

MR. ADAMS having asked for an interview, I had a long conversation with him yesterday at the Foreign Office.

He read me a despatch of Mr. Seward on the subject of the " Alabama" and " Oreto." In this despatch, which was not unfriendly in its tone, Mr. Seward complains of the depredations on American commerce committed by vessels fitted out in British ports, and manned, for the most part, by British sailors. He alludes to the strong feeling excited in the United States by the destruction of her trading vessels and their cargoes. He repeats the complaint common in America that England is at war with the United States, while the United States were not at war with England. He expresses his hope that Great Britain, in execution of her own laws, will put an end to the fitting out of such vessels to prey on the commerce of a friendly nation.

I said that the phrase that England was at war with America, but America was not at war with England, was rather a figure of rhetoric than a true description of facts. That the facts were that two vessels, the " Oreto" and the " Alabama," had eluded the operation of the Foreign Enlistment Act, and had, against the will and purpose of the British Government, made war upon American commerce in the American seas. That the fitting out of the " Alabama," the operation against which the Foreign Enlistment Act was specially directed, was carried on in Portuguese waters at a great distance from any British port. That the most stringent orders had been given long ago to watch the proceedings of those who might be suspected of fitting out vessels of war for Confederate purposes. That if there were six vessels, as it was alleged, fitting out in British ports for such purposes, let evidence be forthcoming, and the Government would not hesitate to stop the vessels, and to bring the offenders before a Court of Justice. That Mr. Adams was no doubt aware that the Government must proceed according to the regular process of law and upon sworn testimony.

Mr. Adams, on the other hand, dwelt on the novelty and enormity of this species of warfare. He said that if a belligerent could fit out in the ports of a neutral swift armed vessels to prey upon the commerce of its adversary, the commerce of that belligerent must be destroyed, and a new and terrible element of warfare would be introduced. He was sure that England would not suffer such conduct on the part of France, nor France on the part of England. He should be sorry to see letters of marque issued by the President; but there might be no better resource than such a measure.

I said I would at once suggest a better measure. Mr. Seward had said to Lord Lyons that the crews of privateers had this advantage—that they reaped the whole benefit of the prizes they took, whereas the crews of men-of-war were entitled to only half the value of the prizes they took. Let the President, I said, offer a higher reward for the capture of the " Alabama " and " Oreto " to the crews of men-of-war than even the entire value of those vessels. Let him offer double their value as a gratuity, and thus confine his action to officers and men of the United States' navy, over whom he could keep a control, and who were amenable to the laws which govern an honourable profession. But what could Mr. Adams ask of the British Government ? What was his proposal ?

Mr. Adams said there was one thing which might be easily done. It was supposed the British Government were indifferent to these notorious violations of their own laws. Let them declare their condemnation of all such infractions of law.

With respect to the law itself, Mr. Adams said either it was sufficient for the purposes of neutrality, and then let the British Government enforce it ; or it was insufficient, and then let the British Government apply to Parliament to amend it.

I said that the Cabinet were of opinion that the law was sufficient ; but that legal evidence could not always be procured. That the British Government had done everything in its power to execute the law ; but I admitted that the cases of the " Alabama " and " Oreto " were a scandal, and in some degree a reproach to our laws. Still, I said, it was my belief that if all the assistance given to the Federals by British subjects, and British munitions of war, were weighed against similar aid given to the Confederates, the balance would be greatly in favour of the Federals.

Mr. Adams totally denied this proposition. But above all, he said, there is a manifest conspiracy in this country, of which the Confederate loan is an additional proof, to produce a state of exasperation in America, and thus bring on a war with Great Britain with a view to aid the Confederate cause, and secure a monopoly of the trade of the Southern States, whose independence these conspirators hope to establish by these illegal and unjust measures. He had worked to the best of his power for peace, but it had become a most difficult task.

Mr. Adams fully deserves the character of having always laboured for peace between our two nations, nor, I trust, will his efforts and those of the two Governments fail of success.

I am, &c.

(Signed)   RUSSELL.

No. 4.

Mr. Adams to Earl Russell.—(Received April 4.)

My Lord,   *Legation of the United States, London, April 4, 1863.*

I HAVE the honour to submit to your consideration the copy of an affidavit voluntarily made by Clarence R. Yonge, being in the nature of accumulative evidence to show the execution of a deliberate plan to establish within the limits of this kingdom a system of action in direct hostility to the Government of the United States. This appears to corroborate in all essential particulars the evidence heretofore adduced from other quarters.

I append the copy of a paper marked A, showing the extent to which Her Majesty's subjects, many of them alleged to belong to the Naval Reserve, have been enlisted in a single example of illegal enterprize.

I pray, &c.

(Signed)   CHARLES FRANCIS ADAMS.

Inclosure in No. 4.

Affidavit of Clarence Randolph Yonge.

I, CLARENCE RANDOLPH YONGE, citizen of the State of Georgia, in the United States, late paymaster on board the steamer "Alabama," formerly called the "290," and also called the "Eurica," and which was built by Messrs. Laird, at Birkenhead, in England, make oath and say as follows:—

I came to England in the steamer "Annie Childs," which sailed from Wilmington, in North Carolina, early in February 1862, and landed in England on or about the 11th of March, 1862, and remained at Liverpool until the steamer "Alabama" went to sea. I came over for the express purpose of acting as paymaster to the "Alabama." I engaged for that purpose with Captain James D. Bullock, at Savannah, Georgia. He had full authority from the Confederate Government in the matters about to be mentioned. Lieutenant North had been sent over to England by the Confederate Government to get iron-clad vessels built. Captain Bullock had been over previously, and had made the contracts for building the "Oreto", and the "Alabama," and was returning to England to assume the command of the latter ship. He was directed at the time to assist Lieutenant North with his advice and experience in building the iron-clads, which Lieutenant North had been sent over here expressly to get built. I was in the Naval Paymaster's Office in Savannah, Georgia, under the Confederate Government. Captain Bullock wanted some one to accompany him, and I was recommended by the paymaster at Savannah to Captain Bullock. I was then released by the paymaster from my engagement, and was subsequently appointed by Captain Bullock, under the written authority of Mr. S. R. Mallory, the Secretary of the Navy, a paymaster in the Confederate Navy, and assigned to the "Alabama." I continued as paymaster in the navy of the Confederate States of America from the time of my appointment in Savannah, Georgia, up to the time of my leaving the "Alabama" at Port Royal in January 1863. The date of my appointment as pay-master in the Confederate Navy was the 21st of December, 1861. Previous to this time I had attended to Captain Bullock's correspondence with the Confederate Government, and I therefore knew that these two vessels, afterwards called the " Oreto " and the " Alabama," were being built in England for the Confederate Government, and by the same means I knew that Captain Bullock, who is a Commander in the Confederate Navy, was the acknow-ledged agent of the Confederate Government for the purpose of getting such ships built. There was some correspondence which I saw between Captain Bullock and Mr. S. R. Mallory, the Secretary of the Navy, relative to purchasing two English vessels which had been used as transports in the Crimean war, Captain Bullock advising against purchasing them as being unfit for the service for which they were required. I wrote the letters from Captain Bullock (and which he signed) to the Secretary advising against this purchase. There was correspondence between Mr. Mallory and Captain Bullock (which I saw and copied) to the effect that the money would be ready and lodged in England to pay for these vessels as it fell due. From what I know I am satisfied that the money was all duly paid as it fell due for these vessels. I saw a letter from Captain Bullock to Fraser, Trenholm and Co. (a firm in Liverpool hereinafter again referred to) thanking them. Captain Bullock kept copies of his correspondence, and they are deposited in one of the banks in Savannah.

From the time of my coming to England until I sailed in the " Alabama" my principal business was in paying the officers of the Confederate Navy, who were over here attached to the " Alabama," and sent over for that purpose. I used to pay them monthly, about the 1st of the month, at Fraser, Trenholm and Co.'s office in Liverpool, and I drew the money for that purpose from that firm.

Commander James D. Bullock, John Low, lieutenant, Eugene Maffitt, midshipman, E. M. Anderson, midshipman, came over to England in the same vessel with myself. Captain Bullock came over to England, in the first instance, to contract for building the two vessels, the " Oreto," now called the " Florida," and the " Alabama." He came to contract for and in behalf of the Southern Confederacy, with the understanding that he was to have the command of one of the vessels. I have heard him say so ; and I have learned this also from the correspondence between him and Mr. Mallory, Secretary of the Confederate Navy, as before mentioned, which passed through my hands.

At the commencement of my engagement with Captain Bullock I acted as his clerk. The contract for building the " Alabama" was made with Messrs. Laird, of Birkenhead, by Captain Bullock. I have seen it myself. I made a copy from the original. The copy was in the ship. It was signed by Captain Bullock, on the one part, and Messrs. Laird, on the other. I made the copy at instance of Captain Bullock from the original, which he has. The ship cost, in United States' money, about 255,000 dollars ; this included provisions, &c., enough for a voyage to the East Indies, which Messrs. Laird were by the contract to provide. The payments were all made before the vessel sailed to the best of my belief. Sinclair, Hamilton and Co., of London, had money. Fraser, Trenholm and Co., of Liver-pool, had money. There was Government money in both their hands over here enough for the purpose of paying them. I was over to see the " Alabama " before she was launched from Messrs. Laird's yard, and was on board the vessel with Captain Bullock, and have met Captain Bullock and one of the Messrs. Laird at Fraser, Trenholm and Co.'s office. Captain Bullock superintended the building of the " Alabama" and " Oreto ;" also whilst he was here Captain Matthew J. Butcher was the captain who took her to sea. He is an Englishman, and represented himself as belonging to the Royal Naval Reserve. At the time the " Alabama " was being built by Messrs. Laird, and when I saw them at different times at their yard in Birkenhead and at Fraser, Trenholm and Co.'s office, I have not the slightest doubt that they perfectly well knew that such steamer was being built for the Southern Confederacy, and that she was to be used in war against the Government of the United States. When the vessel sailed from Liverpool she had her shot racks fitted in the usual places ; she had sockets in her decks, and the pins fitted which held fast frames on carriages for the pivot guns, and breaching bolts. These had been placed in by the builders of the vessel, Messrs. Laird and Co. She was also full of provisions and stores enough for four months' cruise. When she sailed she had beds, bedding, cooking utensils, and mess utensils for 100 men, and powder tanks fitted in.

We sailed from Liverpool on the 29th day of July, 1862. This was some three or four days sooner than we expected to sail. The reason for our sailing at this time before we contemplated, was on account of information which we had received, that proceedings were being commenced to stop the vessel from sailing. Captain Bullock sent Lieutenant Law to me on Sunday evening the 27th of July, to say that I must be at Fraser, Trenholm and Co.'s office early next morning. The next morning I arrived at half-past

9 o'clock. Captain Butcher came in and told me the ship which at that time was called the "290," also "Eurica," would sail the next day, and he wanted me to go with him. In a few minutes Captain Bullock came in and told me he wanted me to go to sea at a minute's notice, that they were going to send her right out. I placed my things on the vessel on that evening. There were about seventy or eighty men in the vessel at this time under Captain Butcher, who had been in command of the vessel for more than a month before she sailed.

I went on the vessel on the morning of the 29th of July, for the purpose of sailing. We started out of the River Mersey at about half-past 10 o'clock. Captain Butcher commanded; Mr. Low acted as first mate; George T. Fullam as second mate; and David Herbert Llewellyn as assistant surgeon.

Captain Bullock, Lieutenants North and Sinclair were on board, also the two Messrs. Laird, Mr. A. E. Byrne, and five or six ladies (including two Miss Lairds), and some other gentlemen whom I do not know. When we sailed it was not our intention to return, but it was with the intention of going to sea, and so understood by us all. The ladies and passengers were taken on board as a blind.

After we got on board, one of the Messrs. Laird who built the vessel came to me and gave me 312l. in English gold. Captain Bullock came and asked me if Mr. Laird had given me the money; that he had some to give me which I must put in the safe. I told him I had not received it, and went to Mr. Laird and got it. Mr. Laird counted it out for me, and I gave him a receipt for the amount. Mr. Laird gave me a number of bills and receipts at the same time for things he had been purchasing for the vessel—beds, blankets, tin ware, knives, forks, for the ship; all of which he (Mr. Laird) had purchased from various parties on account of the ship. My understanding was that the money given me was the balance of the money left, after making these purchases. The bills and receipts which Mr. Laird gave me on this occasion, on account of the purchases he had made, were left on the ship, and were handed over by me to Francis L. Galt, who has succeeded me as paymaster on the ship.

There was a tug-boat in attendance when we left Liverpool on the 29th of July, in which the ladies and all the passengers left. We ran down immediately for Moelfra Bay and lay there all that night, all the next day and next night, until 3 o'clock on Friday morning. I copied a letter of instructions from Captain Bullock to Captain Butcher, in which Captain Butcher was directed to proceed to Porto Praya in Terceira, one of the Azores, where it was intended that we should go to receive the armament. I knew, and all the officers knew, before we went on board that this vessel had been built for the purpose, and was to go out with the intention of cruizing and making war against the Government and people of the United States. This, as I verily believe, was well known by the Messrs. Laird who built her and helped to fit her out, and by Fraser, Trenholm and Co., and by A. E. Byrne of Liverpool, who also assisted in fitting her out, and by Captain Butcher and the other officers who sailed in her.

The next day after we left, the tug-boat "Hercules" came to us from Liverpool about 3 o'clock. She brought to us Captain Bullock and S. G. Porter (who for a time superintended the fitting the vessel), and some two or three men. The men signed articles that night. They had signed articles before at various times while in Liverpool, but they all came up again and renewed the articles. The advance notes had been given them in Liverpool by Captain Butcher, and made payable at Cunard, Wilson and Co. The original articles are now in Fraser, Trenholm and Co.'s office, but in possession of Captain Bullock, who transacts all his business and keeps all his papers at Fraser Trenholm and Co. I do not know the name of the man who acted as shipping master at Liverpool. Captain Bullock wrote a letter of instructions to me before we left Liverpool, directing me to circulate freely among the men, and induce them to go on the vessel after we got to Terceira. I accordingly did circulate among the men on our way out, and persuaded them to join the vessel after we should get to Terceira. Low did the same.

We sailed from Moelfra Bay at 3 o'clock on Friday morning. We went out through the Irish Channel. Captain Bullock left us at the Giant's Causeway. We were some ten or eleven days going out to Terceira. We were in quarantine three days at Porto Praya. There was no transfer of the vessel or anything of the kind there. The barque "Agrippina," from London, arrived there with a part of the armament and all the ammunition, al the clothing and coals. She was commanded by Alexander McQueen. The first day after the arrival of the barque she was getting ready for discharging. This barque is owned by the Confederate Government, but is nominally held by Sinclair, Hamilton, and Co., of London. and sails under the British flag. This firm are connected with the Confederate Government.

Early the following day the barque " Agrippina " hauled alongside, and we commenced to take the guns on board. Two or three days after this the " Bahama " arrived with the officers. This steamer was in command of Captain Tessier. She also sailed under the British flag. The " Bahama " came in, and Captain Butcher went on board, and received orders to sail to Angra. The " Bahama " took the barque in tow, and we all went round to Angra. After we got there we were ordered away by the authorities. There was also correspondence took place between Captain Butcher and the British Consul at that place, but I never heard what it was. We went out, and continued discharging and taking in all that day, and at night we and the barque ran into the bay, the " Bahama " keeping outside. By this time we had got all the guns, ammunition, and cargo from the steamer and barque. During all this time the three vessels were sailing under the British flag. We finished coaling on Sunday, the 24th day of August, about 1 o'clock. We received from the barque " Agrippina " four broadside guns, each 32-pounders. and two pivot-guns, one 68-pounder solid-shot gun, and one 100-pounder rifled gun ; 100 barrels of gunpowder, a number of Enfield rifles, two cases of pistols and cartridges for the same. All the clothing for the men was also received from the " Agrippina," and the fuses, primers, signals, rockets, shot, shell, and other munitions of war needed by the ship ; also a quantity of coal. We received from the " Bahama " two 32-pounder broadside guns, a bale of blue flannel for sailors' wear, and a fire-proof chest with 50,000 dollars in English sovereigns and 50,000 dollars in bank bills.

Captain Butcher or Mr. Low, the First Mate, told me that Mr. M. G. Klingender had been directed to purchase in Liverpool, where Mr. Klingender resides and does business as a merchant, such supplies of tobacco and liquor as were required for the ship's use. I made out the advance notes for the men at Liverpool on the 28th of July, 1862, while she was lying in the Birkenhead docks, which advance notes were made payable by Cunard, Wilson, and Co., at Liverpool ; the half-pay notes which I made out in Moelfra Bay on board the " No. 290 " were made payable at Liverpool by the aforesaid Mr. G. Klingender. After we arrived at Angra, and had armed the ship, and were leaving that port to enter upon the cruize, we were still under the British flag. Captain Semmes then had all the men called aft on the quarter-deck. The British flag was hauled down and the Confederate one raised. He then and there made a speech ; read his Commission to them as a Commander in the Confederate Navy ; told them the objects of the vessel, and what she was about to do ; mentioned to them what their proportion of prize-money would be out of each 100,000 dollars' worth of property captured and destroyed ; said he had on board 100,000 dollars ; and asked them to go with him, at the same time appealing to them as British sailors to aid him in defending the side of the weak.

I had two sets of Articles prepared ; one for men shipping for a limited time, the other for those willing to go during the war. The Articles were then re-signed, while the vessel was in Portuguese waters, but under the Confederate flag. This was on Sunday, the 24th of August, 1862. At the same time Captain Semmes announced that the ship would be called the Confederate States' vessel " Alabama." The guns which were brought out to the " No. 290 " in the " Agrippina " and the " Bahama " were made and furnished by Fawcett, Preston, and Co., of Liverpool. The ammunition and entire armament of the vessel, as well as all the outfit, were purchased in England.

The list hereunto annexed, marked A, contains a list of the names of all the officers on the " Alabama " when I left, except myself, and of all the men whom I can now remember. My belief is that we had eighty-four shipped men, inclusive of the firemen and coal-trimmers, when we left Angra. All the men but three signed the Articles for the period of the war. The half-pay notes were then drawn in favour of and given to the men. These half-pay notes entitled their families or friends to draw half of their pay on the 1st of every month. They were all payable by Fraser, Trenholm, and Co., with whom the money for the purpose of meeting them was lodged. The first set of notes (payable at Cunard, Wilson, and Co.'s) were in the form of the British Marine service ; the second set (payable at Fraser, Trenholm, and Co.'s) were in the form used by the United States' and Confederate Navy. Several of the men refused to sign, and returned in the " Bahama " to Liverpool. Captain Butcher and Captain Bullock also returned in the " Bahama." We then entered upon our cruize.

Out of the eighty-four men I believe there were not more than ten or twelve Americans. There was one Spaniard, and all the rest were Englishmen. More than one-half of the Englishmen belonged to the Royal Navy Reserve, as they informed me, and as was generally understood by all on board. Four at least of the officers were English ; that is to say, John Low, Fourth Lieutenant ; David Herbert Llewellyn, Assistant Surgeon ; George T. Fullam, Master's Mate ; and Henry Allcott, the Sailmaker. I never remember at any time seeing any Custom-house officer aboard this vessel. I remained aboard the vessel as Paymaster from the time I joined her, as before stated, until the 25th day of January, 1863, at which time she was lying at Port Royal, Jamaica. During the whole time that I was on board her she was cruizing and making war against the Government and people of the United States. I cannot recollect the names of all the vessels which she captured, but I know that the number which were captured and destroyed up to the time I left her was at least twenty-three, and, as I believe, was more. Of these twenty-three, four were released upon giving ransom bonds payable to the Confederate Government : such four were, the ship "Emily Farnham," of New York, bound to Liverpool ; the "Tonawanda," of Philadelphia, bound for Liverpool ; the brig "Baron de Custine," bound for the West Indies ; and the mail steam-ship "Ariel," on the Californian line. All the rest were burned or destroyed.

The first port we went into after leaving the Western Islands was Port Royal, Martinique, where we went to provision and coal. The barque "Agrippina" was lying with coals for us, being the same vessel as took out the armament. We did not provision or coal there, but we went out, and afterwards met the "Agrippina" at the Island of Blanco belonging to Venezuela. We only took coal in there. We then proceeded to the Arcas Keys, near Yucatan banks, where we lay about ten days ; where we painted the ship and recoaled from the "Agrippina," and gave the men a run on shore.

We then steered for Galveston, where we destroyed the United States' gun-boat "Hatteras," which was the last vessel we destroyed before I left her.

As soon as we got the prisoners from the "Hatteras" on board we started straight for Jamaica (Port Royal). There we provisioned, coaled, and repaired ship. All the twenty-three ships which we had burned or destroyed had been so burned or destroyed in the interval between our leaving the Western Islands and steering for Port Royal. I heard of no objection from the authorities in Jamaica to our repairing, coaling, or provisioning the ship in Port Royal ; but, on the contrary, we were received with all courtesy and kindness. We were there about a week. Whilst we were there the English Admiral at Port Royal paid a visit to Captain Semmes, on board the "Alabama." I was on shore on duty at the time of the visit, but I heard of such visit immediately upon my return to the ship, for it was the subject of much conversation and remark amongst the officers ; and, in particular, I remember Mr. Sinclair, the master, speaking of it. I also know that Captain Semmes paid a return visit to the English Admiral on the day that the "Alabama" left Port Royal ; I myself saw him start for the purpose. My connection with the ship terminated in Port Royal, and I subsequently came to England, where I arrived on the 22nd of March, 1863.

(Signed)   CLARENCE R. YONGE.

Sworn at the Judge's Chambers, Rolls Gardens, Chancery Lane, this 2nd day of April, 1863.

Before me,
(Signed)   John Payne, *a Commissioner, &c.*

(A.)—*Officers and Crew of the Alabama.*

Raphael Semmes, Commander.
J. M. Kell, First Lieutenant.
Richard F. Armstrong, Second Lieutenant.
Joseph Wilson, Third Lieutenant.
John Low, Fourth Lieutenant, Englishman, sisters living in Liverpool, made his allotment payable to brother-in-law, Charles Green, Jr. Fraser, Trenholm, and Co. pay the men all the allotments, that is, the half-monthly pay. Every month they draw this allotment.
Arthur Sinclair, Master, that is, Sailing Master.
Francis L. Galt, Surgeon, from Virginia, now acting as Paymaster.
Miles J. Freeman, First Assistant Engineer, ranks as Chief. Born in Wales ; does not know whether naturalized.

David Herbert Llewellyn, Assistant Surgeon, Englishman.
B. K. Howell, brother-in-law of Jeff. Davis, Lieutenant of Marines (no marines on board).
Wm. H. Sinclair, Midshipman.
Irvine S. Bullock, Midshipman ; Captain Bullock's brother.
Eugene Maffit, Midshipman ; Captain Maffit's son.
Edward Maffit Anderson, Midshipman ; son of Colonel Anderson.
Wm. P. Brooks, Second Assistant Engineer.
S. W. Cummings, Third Assistant Engineer.
Matthew O'Brien, Third Assistant Engineer.

[87]   C

John M. Pundt, Third Assistant Engineer.

George T. Fullam, First Master's Mate, Englishman; father teacher of Navigation School in Hull.

James Evans, Second Master's Mate, Charleston Pilot.

Wm. B. Smith, Captain's Clerk.

Benj. L. Mecasky, Boatswain.

T. C. Cuddy, Gunner.

William Robinson, Carpenter.

Henry Allcot, Sailmaker, Englishman.

Petty Officers and Seamen.

James King, Master-at-Arms, Savannah Pilot.

Adolphus Marmelstein, Signal Quartermaster, Savannah Pilot.

Wm. A. King, Quartermaster, Savannah Pilot.

James G. Dent, Quartermaster, Savannah Pilot.

Wm. Forestall, Quartermaster, Savannah Pilot.

Ralph Masters, Quarter Gunner.

Wm. Crawford, Quarter Gunner, Royal Naval Reserve, England.

George Addison, Armourer.

Wm. Rinton, Carpenter's Mate, Englishman.

Edward Rawes, Ship's Carpenter, Englishman.

George Harwood, Chief Boatswain's Mate, English Reserve; English Government pay him a pension; time up February 24, 1863 (as he states).

Michael Genshla, Fireman; has a pension in England; has been discharged, November 25, 1862, Irishman.

Brent Johnson, Second Boatswain's Mate, English Reserve.

Wm. Pundy, Sailmaker's Mate, English.

John Latham, Fireman, English.

David Roach, Fireman, English.

Thomas Murphy, Fireman, English.

John McAlee, Ordinary Seaman, English.

Thos. Welsh, Ordinary Seaman, English.

James Smith, Captain of the Forecastle, English.

Edwd. Fitzsmorris, Ordinary Seaman, English.

George Egerton, Fireman, lives at Liverpool, English.

James McFaden, Fireman; time up, 24th February, 1863, English.

Wm. Robinson, Able Seaman, English.

Martin Molk, Able Seaman, English.

Geo. Yeoman, Ordinary Seaman, English.

Wm. McGinley, Able Seaman, English.

George Freemantle, Able Seaman, English.

Frederick Johns, Purser's Steward, English.

John Grady, Boy, uncle lives at 56, Regent-street, Liverpool, Bootmaker, English.

Thos. Weir, Gunner's Mate, English.

James Brasner, Able Seaman, English.

Edgar Fripp, Seaman, English.

John Neil, Seaman, English.

Joseph Neil, Seaman, English.

Samuel Henry, Seaman, English.

John Roberts, Seaman, English.

John Duggan, Seaman, English.

Martin King, Seaman, English.

F. Williams, Seaman, English.

R. Williams, Seaman, English.

Joseph Pearson, Seaman, English.

Joseph Connor, Seaman, English.

Thos. McMillan, Seaman, English.

Michael Mars, Seaman, English.

Robert Egan, Boy, English.

Malcolm McFarlane, Seaman, English.

Peter Henry, Seaman, English.

Charles Godwin, Seaman, American.

James Higgs, Captain of Hold, English.

Peter Duncan, Fireman, English.

Richard Parkinson Ward, Purser's Steward, English.

George Appleby, Yeoman, English.

John Enwry, Seaman, English.

Wm. Heam, Seaman, English.

Thos. L. Parker, Boy, English.

A. G. Bartelli, Captain's Steward, American.

Peter Hughes, Seaman, American.

Henry Fisher, Seaman, belonging to Reserve, English.

Frank Townsend, Seaman, belonging to Reserve, English.

Frank Cunen, Seaman, belonging to Reserve, English.

William Levins, Coal Trimmer, English.

There are now several men on board of the " Alabama" who have joined the ship since we entered upon the cruize, some of whom are Americans.

(Signed)   CLARENCE R. YONGE.

This is the list marked A referred to in the Affidavit of Clarence Randolph Yonge, sworn this 2nd day of April, 1863.

Before me,

(Signed)   JOHN PAYNE, *a Commissioner, &c.*

No. 5.

Mr. Adams to Earl Russell.—(Received April 30.)

My Lord,   *Legation of the United States, London, April 29,* 1863.
I AM directed by the Government of the United States to submit to your consideration a copy of a Memorial addressed to the President by the directing authorities of the
Panama Railroad Company. I am further instructed to say that this case is regarded as
coming within the category described in my note to your Lordship of the 20th of November
last, touching the depredations committed by gun-boat No. 290, now known as the
"Alabama," but attended by some peculiar circumstances fully set forth in the Memorial
itself.

I pray &c.
(Signed)   CHARLES FRANCIS ADAMS.

Inclosure 1 in No. 5.

The President and Secretary of the Panama Railroad Company to the President of the United States.

Office of the Panama Railroad Company, New York,
Sir,   *March* 14, 1863.
THE Undersigned, President and Secretary of the Panama Railroad Company, beg
leave to make the following statements:—
1. That the American barque "Golden Rule," of the registered tonnage of 254$\frac{70}{95}$ tons,
hereinafter mentioned, was the property of the said Panama Railroad Company and others.
2. That the said barque, while on her voyage from the port of New York to the port
of Aspinwall or Colon, in New Granada, was captured on the 26th day of January last by
the steamer "Alabama," of the so-called Confederate States of America, in about 75° west
longitude, and 18° north latitude, and after the removal of a portion of her cargo to the
"Alabama," was totally destroyed by burning, together with the residue of her cargo
remaining on board.
3. That the value of the barque "Golden Rule," with her freight, was 16,000 dollars,
and that of the cargo she had on board the Panama Railroad Company was owner to the
amount of 1,406 dollars.
4. That the aforesaid steamer "Alabama" was built in England, and sailed from a
British port after notice had been given Her Majesty's Government that she was intended
to be employed in the service of the so-called Confederate States of America, as a vessel of
war, to operate against the commerce of the United States.
5. That the destruction of the barque "Golden Rule" by the steamer "Alabama"
took place within twenty-four hours after the departure of the "Alabama" from
Port Royal, in the Island of Jamaica, a Colonial port of Great Britain, where she had
been permitted to remain during the whole of the preceding five days for the purpose of
repairing, refitting, coaling, and provisioning.
6. That the cargo on board the "Golden Rule" was owned to a great extent by
neutral parties of various nationalities, among whom are British subjects, and that the
citizens of Great Britain are largely interested in the Panama Railroad Company, both as
owners of the sterling bonds and of the shares of the Company.
In view of the foregoing facts, the Undersigned consider the Government of Great
Britain to be justly bound to make good to the Panama Railroad Company and others the
loss sustained by the destruction of the barque "Golden Rule," and of the cargo on board
belonging to said Company, say to the aggregate amount of 17,406 dollars, and they
respectfully request your Excellency to take such measures to obtain redress as in your
judgment may seem best.
(Signed)   DAVID HOADLEY, *President.*
JAS. F. JOY, *Secretary.*

Inclosure 2 in No. 5.

Memorial.
New York, March 14, 1863.
THE Undersigned, citizens of the United States, being duly sworn, depose and
say:—
That they were master and first officer of the American barque "Golden Rule,"
C 2

belonging to the Panama Railroad Company and others, on her late voyage from the port of New York to Aspinwall, or Colon, in New Granada; that on the 26th day of January last, whilst becalmed near the longitude of 75° west, and latitude 18° north, the said barque was captured by the steamer " Alabama," of the so-called Confederate States of America, commanded by Captain Semmes; that on going on board the " Alabama," the Commander was informed that the cargo of the " Golden Rule " was owned in part by neutral parties, probably to the extent of one-fourth or one-third; that after the removal of a portion of the cargo to the " Alabama," the barque was set on fire by order of the Commander of the " Alabama," and totally destroyed, together with the cargo remaining on board.

(Signed)   P. H. WHITEBURN, *Master*, "*Golden Rule.*"

JOHN CASSIDY, *Officer*, "*Golden Rule.*"

State of New York, City and County of New York, ss.

Be it known that on the 14th day of March, A.D, 1863, before me, Frederick Bull, a Notary Public in and for the State of New York, duly commissioned and sworn, dwelling in the city of New York, personally came David Hoadley, President, and Joseph F. Joy, Secretary of the Panama Railroad Company, and P. H. Whiteburn, master, and John Cassidy, first officer, of the American barque " Golden Rule," to me known, who being severally sworn, did each for himself depose and say, that the foregoing statements by them respectively subscribed are correct and true, to the best of their knowledge and belief.

In witness whereof, I have hereunto set my hand, and affixed my notarial seal, the day and year last before written.

(Signed)   FREDERICK BULL, *Notary Public*, 58, *Wall Street.*

No. 6.

Earl Russell to Mr. Adams.

Sir,   *Foreign Office, April* 30, 1863.

I HAVE the honour to acknowledge the receipt of your letter of the 29th instant, inclosing a Memorial addressed to the President of the United States, by the directing authorities of the Panama Railroad Company, respecting the destruction by the " Alabama " of the American barque " Golden Rule."

I am, &c.

(Signed)   RUSSELL.

No. 7.

Mr. Adams to Earl Russell.—(*Received July* 8.)

My Lord,   *Legation of the United States, London, July* 7, 1863.

AS constituting one of the claims of citizens of the United States growing out of the lawless depredations upon American commerce by vessels fitted out and sent from the ports of Great Britain, I am directed to transmit to your Lordship copies of the papers herewith submitted (Inclosures 1 and 2).

I have the honour at the same time to annex copies of two other depositions furnished to me from the Consul of the United States at Liverpool, relating to the same general subject (Inclosures 3 and 4).

It is with great regret that I feel myself once more compelled to call your Lordship's attention to the circumstance attending the outfit of the steamer called the "Japan." It now appears that that vessel was at the time of her escape, and has continued until very lately to be, the property of a British subject residing in Liverpool. That person is Mr. Thomas Bold, a member of the commercial house of Jones and Co. I have information which leads me to believe that only within a few days has Mr. Bold notified the Collector of Customs at Liverpool of his sale of this vessel to foreign owners, and requested the register to be cancelled. That act was not completed until the 23rd of June last. It would appear from these facts, should they prove to be true, that this vessel has remained the property of a British subject during a considerable time in which she has been engaged in committing extensive ravages upon the commerce of a nation with which Her Majesty is at peace. The fact of the outfit of that vessel for hostile purposes has already occupied the attention of your Lordship, in consequence of former representations unhappily made too late for effective interposition. But the circumstances of the retention of the ownership by a British subject for so long a period after she was known to be engaged in hostilities against the United States, is of too grave a character to justify me in omitting to call your Lordship's particular attention to it in advance of the possibility of receiving instructions respecting it.

I pray, &c.

(Signed)   CHARLES FRANCIS ADAMS.

Inclosure 1 in No. 7.

Messrs. Robinson, Howard, and McGaw to Mr. Seward.

Sir,   New York, June 4, 1863.

THE Undersigned, owners of the ship "Golden Eagle" and her freight, beg to state that on the 21st February last that vessel was captured and burned by the steamer "Alabama," a vessel built in an English port, the particulars of which are fully set forth in the notarial copy of the protest of her master herewith, and to which we beg your attention.

	Dollars.
The value of the vessel was	36,000
Freight 3,600*l.* sterling, at 67½ per cent.	26,800
Our loss	62,800

Believing we have a good and valid claim against the English Government for this loss, we have to ask your kind offices in the premises; and would feel obliged if you will take such steps as will best protect our interests, and we remain, &c.,

(Signed)   EDWIN H. ROBINSON.
             H. L. HOWARD, *Executrix of B. Howard's Estate.*
             JOHN H. McGAW.

Inclosure 2 in No. 7.

Protest.

Consulate of the United States of America, London.

TO all whom it may concern, be it known and made manifest, that on this 24th day of March, in the year of our Lord 1863, before me, Freeman H. Morse, Consul of the United States of America for London and the dependencies thereof, personally appeared Edward A. Swift, master and commander of the ship "Golden Eagle" of New Bedford, United States aforesaid, of the burden of 1,120⅗ tons or thereabouts. And the said Edward A. Swift having before on the 20th day of March, within twenty-four hours after his arrival declared to protest before me, John Britton, United States' Consul at Southampton; now comes being desirous to extend the same before me, and with him come Carl Brown, second officer; John Smith, Carpenter; John Smith, A. Gates, Thomas Parker, E. Huboard, W. Gibson, M. Gilford, A. Silvé, J. Francis, John Leons, T. Whiskey, Merritt D. Bradley, W. L. Cartons, H. Dodson, and George Burrill, seamen, being duly sworn on the Holy Evangelists of Almighty God, before me the said Consul, did declare and set forth as follows, that is to say, that they the said appearers and the said ship's company sailed in and with the said ship from the port of Howland's Island on the 23rd of November now last past, with a cargo of guano bound to the port of Cork for orders, the said ship being tight, staunch, and strong, and in all respects in good order, and well fitted for the said voyage.

That nothing material occurred until the 21st February, on which day at 10 A.M, being then in latitude 29° 17' north, and longitude 45° 15' west, on the starboard tack, by the wind, saw a sail on the port bow standing towards us. At 11 A.M. spoke the barque "Olive Jane" of Boston for New York. At 11·30 A.M. made the sail on the port bow to be a gun-boat and a steamer by her smoke pipe, distance about six miles (which proved to be the pirate steamer "Alabama"). Soon after she fired two blank shots, having the Confederate flag at her peak, and tacking ship as ourselves, the wind being very light at the time and the ship going about four miles per hour, the steamer soon took in sail and steamed down upon us, firing a shot which fell short of the ship. About 1·15 P.M., the steamer fired again, the shot passing close ahead of the ship. At 1·30 p.m., finding they were preparing to fire again, appearers brought the ship to. An armed boat's crew boarded and took possession. At 6 P.M., the "Alabama" having chased another vessel (the barque "Olive Jane"), and set fire to her returned to the ship. Appearer Swift was ordered on board with the ship's papers. Captain Semmes giving orders to the first Lieutenant to plunder and burn the ship, they taking all the ship's papers, chronometer, two sextants, spy glasses, charts, books, log-book, and all appearer Swift's private property with the exception of a small quantity of clothes, and allowing the appearers, the officers and crew, a small bag of clothes each, and upon arrival on the " Alabama," they were placed in irons on deck all the time, with the exception of said appearer Swift who was taken below and searched, and the little money, about 157 dollars, taken away from him, he being allowed to mess and sleep in the steerage with the petty officers. At 5 P.M., the " Golden Eagle " was set fire to, and at 8 A.M. on the 22nd went down, the steamer remaining by the burning ship all night. On the 27th, the " Alabama " gave chase to the ship " Washington " bound from Callao to Antwerp, and after boarding her and finding her cargo owned by foreigners, took bonds for her, and put appearers and other persons upon her. Appearers remained six days on the " Alabama."

On the 18th March, the " Washington " spoke Cowes pilot-boat No. 3, off the Isle of Wight, south south-west, and placed appearers and other sufferers on board, and they made for Cowes, where they arrived and were put on shore.

Now, therefore, be it known that they, the said appearers, have protested, and by these presents do protest, against the said pirate No. 290, *alias* the " Alabama," commanded by Captain Semmes, her officers and crew, as the sole cause of all losses, costs, and damages that the said ship " Golden Eagle " or her cargo have suffered, or may suffer by reason thereof.

(Signed)	Edward A. Swift, *Master*.	(Signed)	John Francis.
	Carl Brown, *Second Officer*.		John Leon.
	John Smith, *Carpenter*.		Thom. Whiskey.
	Thom. Smith.		John Williams.
	Andrew Gates.		Charley Browne.
	Thos. P. Parker.		Cruz Calloha.
	Elisha Hubbard.		James Badger.
	William Gibson.		Isaac De Merritt.
	Matthew Gilford.		David Bradley.
	Antonio Silvé.		Wm. L. Curtions.
	Henry Dodson.		George Burrill.

In testimony of all which I the said Consul have hereunto set my hand and affixed my seal of office in London, the day and year first herein mentioned, and in the eighty-seventh year of the independence of the said United States.
(Signed)   F. H. MORSE.

Consulate of the United States of America, London.
I, Freeman H. Morse, Consul to the United States of America for London and the dependencies thereof, do hereby certify to all to whom it may concern, that the foregoing is a true and faithful copy of a certain Instrument of Protest of the ship " Golden Eagle," of New Bedford, made and extended before me on the 24th day of March, and taken from the registry of the office of this Consulate in book marked " Record Book of Protest No. 5," at folio 17.

In testimony whereof I have hereunto set my hand and affixed my seal of office at London, this 24th day of March, in the year of our Lord 1863, and in the 87th year of the Independence of the said United States.
(Signed)   F. H. MORSE.

City and County of New York, ss.
I, Andrew Foster Higgins, a Public Notary in and for the said city and county, duly commissioned and sworn, do hereby certify the foregoing to be a true and exact copy of a certified copy of protest exhibited to me.

In testimony whereof I hereunto set my hand and seal of office this 2nd day of June, A.D. 1863.
(Signed)   A. F. HIGGINS, *Notary Public.*

Inclosure 3 in No. 7.

Affidavit of John Trader.

I, JOHN TRADER, at present on board the barque " Regatta," now lying in the Queen's dock in Liverpool in the county of Lancaster, seaman, make oath and say :—
On the 18th day of March last I joined at Baltimore the barque " Henrietta," Captain

13

Brown, master, as boy on a voyage from Baltimore to Rio, with a cargo of flour, and two gentlemen and one lady, with three children, as passengers.

We left Baltimore on the 20th of March, and proceeded on our voyage, and on the 23rd of April, when about fifty-six miles south of the Equator, we were becalmed, and about 4 o'clock in the afternoon we saw a strange vessel astern of us; she had all her sails furled, and appeared to be making towards us under steam, and between 5 and 6 o'clock she came up to us, and when about forty to fifty yards from us, she hailed us and asked where we were bound to and where from. Our captain told him. The strange vessel was flying the American colours, the officer on board the strange vessel sang out to back our mainyard, and he would send some one on board. We backed the mainyard, and the stranger then sent off a boat which came alongside of us. An officer and several men then came on board ; they were all armed with revolvers and swords ; they told us to get ready to go on board of their vessel. All the seamen of the " Henrietta," except myself, went into the boat, and were taken to the stranger. Another boat then came off from the stranger and took me; the two mates, and the steward, off to the ship. When we got on board the stranger we were put into irons, and remained on deck. We found some ten or twelve prisoners ; they were all in irons. Another boat was sent from the stranger and fetched the captain and passengers, and they were brought on board, but they were not put in irons. Our mates were put into irons at first, but they were afterwards taken off.

About one hour after we came on board the stranger we saw our ship was on fire, and I also noticed that the stranger was flying the Southern colours, and that the American colours she had been flying when she hailed us had been hauled down, and about this time I heard that the stranger was the "Florida."

When the fire had got a good hold of the " Henrietta," the " Florida " steamed away and then lay-to for the night.

On the following morning we got up steam and steamed down towards our vessel which we passed ; she was then nearly burnt down to the water's edge. After cruizing about we saw a strange sail, and made for her. She was an English vessel bound, I think, for Liverpool. One of the officers of the " Florida " hailed her, and asked her master if he could take any passengers ; he said yes, but he would want a barrel of bread and a barrel of beef to be put on board first for every one taken. We then steamed off, and about 8 or 9 o'clock in the morning we saw another sail, and in about two or three hours we came up with her. She was hailed, and turned out to be an American ship called the " Oneida," bound to New York from Shanghae with tea. The " Florida " was flying the American colours. The " Oneida " was ordered to lie-to, and a boat was sent off from the " Florida " to the " Oneida " with an armed crew. We were on deck and could see what took place. When the boat's crew had got on board the " Oneida " the " Florida " hoisted the Southern flag, and the " Oneida " hauled down her American flag ; the " Florida's " boats brought off the captain and crew of the " Oneida." The crew were put into irons immediately they came on board. The " Oneida " was then set fire to. When the fire had got good hold of the vessel we steamed away from her, and continued to cruize about. We then saw another sail, which we made for, and on coming up to her we found she was a French barque bound to New South Wales. She was hailed by one of the officers of the " Florida," and told to back her mainyards. We could not make him understand. A boat was sent off to her, and Captain Brown, our captain, and one of our men, Peter Brown, who went as an interpreter, went on board. Our captain told us he was going to see if he could get a passage for all, himself and his crew and passengers. In about half-an-hour our captain returned and told us that the Frenchman would only take six, and the captain and the mates and passengers and the captain of the " Oneida " went on board the Frenchman. The seamen Peter Brown also remained on board the Frenchman. After we got rid of these parties we proceeded to cruize about again, and on the following morning we came across the Danish brig " Ceres," bound for Gibraltar, and I and H. G. Wagner and William Evans and John Short and the cook were put on board of her. We remained on board of this ship until, her provisions running short, I and Wagner and Evans and Short were put on board the " Regatta," bound for Liverpool, where I arrived yesterday, but Wagner and Evans were put on board the " Inca," also bound for Liverpool, as our water was running short.

(Signed)   JOHN TRADER.

Sworn at Liverpool, in the county of Lancaster, this 5th day of June, 1863.
   Before me,
(Signed)   JOHN YATES, *a Commissioner to Administer Oaths in the Courts of Exchequer or Pleas.*

Affidavit of Henry George Wagner.

I, HENRY GEORGE WAGNER, at present on board the barque "Inca" of Liverpool, now lying in the King's dock in the port of Liverpool, in the county of Lancaster, seaman, make oath and say,—

1. In the month of March last I shipped at Baltimore on board the barque "Henrietta" of Baltimore, G. D. Brown master, for a voyage to Rio. The "Henrietta" was a vessel of 440 tons, and we had a crew of thirteen all told, and a Mr. Roberts, a Mr. Morris, and a lady of the name of Florence with her three children, were passengers.

2. On the 20th March we sailed from Baltimore, and proceeded on our voyage without anything happening until the 23rd of April; we were then about fifty-six miles south of the Equator, and were becalmed, when at 4 in the afternoon we saw a strange sail to the stern of us. The stranger had no sails set but was under steam, and about 5 or 6 o'clock the stranger came up with us. She had the American flag flying at the fore royal mast-head, and nothing at the peak. She hailed us, and asked us where we were from, and where bound to. We told him, and he then sung out to us to back our mainyard, and he would send his boat alongside. Captain Brown refused to back his mainyard. The stranger then lowered three boats, and came alongside and boarded us. There were four officers and twelve men. They were all armed with revolvers and cutlasses.

3. When they came on board, they asked Captain Brown for his papers and irons. The captain said he had no papers, but he told them where the irons were. Captain Brown was then ordered into one of the boats, and the two mates and the passengers also went into the same boat on board the stranger. I and the rest of the crew of the "Henrietta" were then ordered into another of the boats, and were rowed to the stranger. When we got under her stern, the stranger hoisted the Southern flag. We then went on board the stranger, and I and the rest of the seamen were put in irons.

4. The other of the stranger's boats brought the captain and the passengers' clothes, chronometer, charts, and other things, but they did not bring our things. I only got an old shirt and a pair of old trousers beyond what I stood up in, when taken out of my ship.

5. After the boats had all come from our ship, and we had been on board about an hour and a quarter, I saw the flames coming up out of the cabin windows of the "Henrietta," and I then knew she had been fired. The stranger as soon as she saw the ship was burning put off from her, and went about ten miles away and then laid-to.

6. We were on deck, and could see our ship burning until about 3 in the morning, when the fire went out about half-past 5 or 6 o'clock. The stranger, whose name we now learned was the "Florida," steamed past our vessel, which was burned almost to the water's edge.

7. After we had passed our ship the "Florida" continued to cruise about, and just afterwards we hailed a strange sail, which turned out to be an English barque, bound to Liverpool from Buenos Ayres. The Captain of the "Florida" asked him if he would like any passengers, but the master of the barque said he could not do so. We then continued cruizing about flying the American colours, and about 8 o'clock on the 24th of April a sail was seen to the north-west of us, and we then made for her and overhauled her about 10 o'clock. She was hailed, and answered that she was the "Oneida" of New Bedford, bound to New York from Shanghae, and loaded with tea. The Captain of the "Florida" then ordered three boats and crew to go on board of the "Oneida," which they did, and after bringing the captain and crew of sixteen in all on board, the ship was set fire to. We lay by until the lower sails had caught, and the "Florida" then steamed away.

8. In the afternoon of the same day we spoke a strange barque which turned out to be from Bordeaux bound for New South Wales, and one of the "Florida's" boats took Captain Brown, one of the crew of the "Henrietta," Peter Brown, and went on board the Frenchman. Our captain told us he was going to see if the French captain would take all of us and the passengers on board. When our captain came back, he told us that the Frenchman could not take the crew, but that he, the master and passengers and one of the boys, the captain's son, and the captain and mate of the "Oneida," were going on board, and they subsequently went on board. Peter Brown, one of our seamen, also went on board. He acted as interpreter.

9. The "Florida" after she had put the captain of the "Henrietta" and "Oneida" and the others on board of the Frenchman, laid-to until daylight of the next day, which was the 25th of April. In the morning of that day about 8 o'clock, a strange sail was seen which we made for under all steam, and after running after her for about an hour

and a-half, another sail came in sight, and we then ran for her, and spoke her. She turned out to be the Danish brig " Ceres " bound for Gibraltar for orders. The first Lieutenant of the " Florida " hailed her, and asked her if she could take any passengers. The master of the " Ceres " said he could take five, and the captain of the " Florida " then sent me and John Shutt, and William Evans, John Trader, and our cook, in one of the " Florida's " boats on board the " Ceres." I remained on board the " Ceres " until the 2nd of May, when our provisions running short, the captain of the " Ceres " spoke the English barque "Regatta" bound for Liverpool, and I and William Evans, and John Shutt, and John Trader, were put on board the " Regatta."

10. On the 18th May, the " Regatta's " water running short, I and William Evans were put on board the " Inca," which we had previously spoken, and we arrived in Liverpool yesterday.

During the whole of the time I was in the " Florida," we were left on the deck and in irons, and when we went on board we found some fourteen or fifteen other prisoners.

11. The " Florida " carried two large pivot guns, one forward and one aft, and she had three large guns on each side. The crew was a mixed one, most of them being Irishmen. They numbered I should think about 130. We were asked to join the " Florida," and were offered 22 dollars a month, 50 dollars bounty, and a share of prize money, but we refused to join under any conditions.

(Signed)   HENRY G. WAGNER.

Sworn at Liverpool in the County of Lancaster, this 5th day of June, 1863.

Before me,
(Signed)   JOHN YATES, *a Commissioner for taking Affidavits in the Courts of Exchequer or Pleas.*

No. 8.

Earl Russell to Mr. Adams.

Sir,   *Foreign Office, July* 13, 1863.

I HAVE the honour to acknowledge the receipt of your letter of the 7th instant, inclosing papers relative to the destruction of the American ships " Golden Eagle " and " Henrietta " by the " Alabama " and the " Florida," and calling attention to the circumstance that the " Virginia " continued up to the 23rd ultimo to be the property of a British subject residing at Liverpool.

So far as it may be intended, by the communication of the inclosed papers, to assert or record a claim against Her Majesty's Government on account of the destruction of those vessels, I would beg leave to refer you to my letter of the 9th of March last, and to repeat that Her Majesty's Government entirely disclaim all responsibility for the acts of vessels of war of the so-styled Confederate Government.

I have, however, called for a report from the proper authorities with regard to your statement respecting the " Virginia."

I am, &c.
(Signed)   RUSSELL.

No. 9.

Earl Russell to Mr. Adams.

Sir,   '   *Foreign Office, August* 17, 1863.

MY attention has been called by a member of the firm of Messrs. Fraser, Trenholm, and Co., of Liverpool, to a letter which appeared in the " Daily News " of the 2nd of April last, purporting to be a letter addressed by Mr. Thomas H. Dudley, United States' Consul at Liverpool, to the Collector of Customs at that port.

In that letter it is stated that when the " Alabama " was first tried, Mr. Welsman, one of the firm of Fraser, Trenholm and Co., was present, and that he accompanied that vessel on her various trials, as he had also accompanied the " Oreto " on her trial trip and on her departure.

Mr. Welsman positively denies that he was present when the " Alabama " was first tried, or that he ever accompanied her in any way on any of her supposed trials. He further denies that he ever set foot on board the " Oreto ; " and he has recorded these

[87]   D

denials in an affidavit subscribed and sworn to before the Acting British Consul at Charleston.

With the view of placing Mr. Welsman's statement still further upon record, and as evidence of the incorrectness of Mr. Dudley's assertion, I have the honour to communicate to you the substance of Mr. Welsman's affidavit for the information of your Government.

I am, &c.
(Signed)   RUSSELL.

No. 10.

Mr. Adams to Earl Russell.—(Received August 24.)

My Lord,   *Legation of the United States, London, August 22, 1863.*

I HAVE the honour to acknowledge the reception of your note of the 17th instant, relating to the notice taken by Mr. Welsman, one of the firm of Fraser, Trenholm, and Co., of certain statements made respecting him by Mr. Dudley, the Consul of the United States at Liverpool. I have transmitted a copy of the same for the information of my Government, and another to Mr. Dudley.

I pray, &c.
(Signed)   CHARLES FRANCIS ADAMS.

No. 11.

Mr. Adams to Earl Russell.—(Received August 25.)

My Lord,   *Legation of the United States, London, August 24, 1863.*

I AM directed by my Government to lay before your Lordship copies of a letter and Memorial addressed to the Secretary of State of the United States by Messrs. Upton, claiming indemnity for the destruction of the ship "Nora," burnt at sea by a vessel fitted out and dispatched from the port of Liverpool. I am instructed to request that the substance of this claim may be considered as added to others of the same kind which it has been my painful duty to present to your Lordship heretofore.

I pray, &c.
(Signed)   CHARLES FRANCIS ADAMS.

Inclosure 1 in No. 11.

Messrs. Upton to Mr. Seward.

S ,   *Boston, July 14, 1863.*

WE respectfully inclose a Memorial and Protest in the case of the ship "Nora," burnt at sea by the vessel calling herself the "Alabama."

The general facts are stated in the body of the Memorial, and we therefore refrain from a repetition in this communication.

In most respectfully asking the attention of the Government to this matter, we remain, &c.

(Signed)   GEO. B. UPTON.
                GEO. B. UPTON, Jun.

Inclosure 2 in No. 11.

Protest.

To the Honourable William H. Seward, Secretary of State, Washington, D. C.

THE Memorial of George B. Upton and George B. Upton, Junior, citizens of the United States, residing in Boston, in the State of Massachusetts, sole owners of the American ship "Nora," respectfully represents :—

That said ship, being a legally-registered American ship, left the port of Bangor, in the United States, for the port of Liverpool, in Great Britain, on the 29th day of November, 1862. That said ship arrived in safety at said port of Liverpool, where, after being discharged, she was laden with a cargo upon the charter of Mr. W. N. de Mattos, from said port of Liverpool to Calcutta, the undersigned having no other personal interest in said cargo than the usual lien for the freight thereof; the cargo being, as represented to them, the property of British subjects. Said ship sailed from the port of Liverpool on or about the 15th day of February of the present year, and had proceeded on her voyage as far as latitude 1° 23′ north, longitude 26° 30′ west, when she was boarded by, and declared to be a prize to, a vessel calling herself "the Confederate States' man-of-war ' Alabama,' " who immediately took possession of said ship, against the remonstrance of the master, and who further proceeded to remove sundry stores from said ship; and on the 27th day of March the said ship was set on fire by the order of one Semmes, calling himself the Captain of said steamer, and was totally destroyed ; and said officers and crew were taken from said ship "Nora," and kept on board said piratical steamer "Alabama," from the date of the destruction of said ship until the 16th day of April last past.

And now we, the said George B. Upton, and George B. Upton, Junior, sole owners of said ship, do enter our solemn protest against the destruction thereof, and do by these presents demand of the Government of Great Britain full reparation for the same, in the sum of 80,000 dollars of the coin of the United States, being the value of said ship and freight at the time of her destruction.

Your Memorialists would further represent that they make and predicate this protest and demand upon the facts hereinafter stated, which can be verified whenever it shall be found necessary so to do. Said vessel calling herself "the Confederate States' man-of-war ' Alabama,' " is an English vessel, and no other. She was built at the port of Birkenhead, and was allowed to leave British waters, although information as to her character, and the intention to use her as a privateer to prey upon the commerce of the United States, then and now at peace with Great Britain, was lodged with the British Government. That said steamer "Alabama" (then called the "290"), was allowed to leave said waters upon giving a bond to return, which it was well known was intended to be forfeited. That she did not leave the waters of Great Britain the latter part of July 1862, under the protection of the British flag, and manned by British subjects. That had the American man-of-war "Tuscarora," or any other legally authorized man-of-war of the United States, seized her after leaving said British waters, she would have claimed her British ownership and her flag as her protection. But said steamer was allowed to leave port under the pretence of making a trial trip, and has never been in any port of the so-called "Confederate States," so as to change her flag, or to be otherwise than a British vessel.

Your Memorialists would further represent that said steamer, after thus fraudulently leaving the ports of Great Britain against the Queen's Proclamation of Neutrality, repeatedly visited or came within the jurisdiction of certain British islands in the Atlantic Ocean, when and where it was well known and patent to the world that she had destroyed American vessels on the high seas; and instead of being seized and detained by the British Government, as they were in duty bound to do, was allowed every facility for obtaining supplies and advice, and to resume her piratical cruize. That no examination was ever made by said British Government, through their constituted agents and officers, as to the manning of said steamer by British subjects, or of the prostitution of the British flag by thus giving protection to the piracies committed under its folds; and that she was, and has continued to be, until after the capture of your Memorialists' ship "Nora," principally manned by British subjects.

In view of these matters, and of others which may be made to appear, your Memorialists do now and for ever enter their solemn protests against the British Government and people, as willing parties, negligently culpable, in the destruction of their property on the high seas, and thus in first violating the Proclamation of the Queen by building and manning said steamer, and then allowing her to continue her depredations.

And they ask, through the Government of the United States, that a proper representation may be made of their loss, that in the end due reparation may be made to them by the said Government of Great Britain, or that the Government of the United States may assume the same as one of the Governmental obligations to protect the rights of their citizens, thus wantonly violated.

And as in duty bound will every pray.

(Signed)   GEO B. UPTON.
GEO. B. UPTON, Jun.

Boston, July 14, 1863.

United States of America, Commonwealth of Massachusetts, Suffolk, ss.

Be it known to all whom it doth or may concern, that on this 14th day of July, in the year of our Lord 1863, before me John S. Tyler, a Notary Public and Justice of the Peace, under the great seal of the Commonwealth, duly commissioned and sworn, at my office in the city of Boston, personally came George B. Upton and George B. Upton, Junior, resident merchants of this city, to me well known, and made before me the foregoing memorial and protest, declaring the same to be just and true. Wherefore at the request of the said appearers I have caused the same to be verified by the oaths of said appearers, and to be entered on my notarial record to serve as occasion may require.

In testimony whereof I hereto 'affix my official seal the day of the date above written.

(Signed)   JOHN S. TYLER, *Notary Public and Justice of the Peace.*

No. 12.

Mr. Layard to Mr. Laird, M.P.

Sir,   *Foreign Office, August* 31, 1863.

IN a note which Lord Russell has lately received from Mr. Adams the "Alabama" is described as a vessel "fitted out and despatched from the port of Liverpool," and his Lordship directs me to say that he would feel much obliged to you if you could inform him how far it is true that the "Alabama" was fitted out as a vessel of war at Liverpool before she left that port.

I am, &c.
(Signed)   A. H. LAYARD.

No. 13.

Mr. Laird, M.P., to Mr. Layard.

Sir,   *Birkenhead, September* 2, 1863.

IN reply to your letter of the 31st August, stating that Lord Russell would feel much obliged to me if I can inform him "how far it is true that the 'Alabama' was fitted out as a vessel of war at Liverpool before she left that port," I request that you will inform his Lordship that I am not able from my own personal observation or knowledge to reply to his Lordship's inquiry, as I did not see the "Alabama" after the first week in July 1862, being some weeks before she sailed.

In order to obtain for his Lordship from a reliable source the information he has asked for, I have made inquiries from my successors in business, the firm of Laird Brothers, the builders of the vessel now called the "Alabama," and I am authorised by them to state that the vessel referred to was delivered by them at the port of Liverpool, and that at the time of her delivery she was not fitted out as a vessel of war.

They also confirm in every respect the report of Mr. Morgan, the Surveyor of Customs at Liverpool, dated 30th July, 1862 (ordered by the House of Commons to be printed 24th March, 1863), in which he states that a strict watch had been kept upon the vessel, and that she left the port without any part of her armament on board.

I am, &c.
(Signed)   JOHN LAIRD.

No. 14.

Earl Russell to Mr. Adams.

Sir,   *Foreign Office, September* 14, 1863.

IN acknowledging the receipt of your letter of the 24th ultimo, in which you request that Messrs. Upton's claim on account of the destruction of their vessel the "Nora" by the "Alabama" may be added to others of the same kind which you have heretofore presented to me, I must, on the part of Her Majesty's Government, repeat the disclaimer which on more than one occasion I have already made to you of all responsibility in regard to the proceedings of the "Alabama," or of any other Confederate cruiser.

But, as it is stated in your letter that the "Alabama" was "fitted out and dispatched from the port of Liverpool." and as these words imply that you suppose she was fitted out as a vessel of war, I have thought it right to ask Mr. Laird how far that statement is borne out by the facts, and I have the honour to inclose, for your information, a copy of a letter which I have received from that gentleman in reply,* stating that from the information he had received it appears that the "Alabama" was not fitted out at Liverpool as a vessel of war.

When the United States' Government assumes to hold the Government of Great Britain responsible for the captures made by vessels which may be fitted out as vessels of war in a foreign port because such vessels were originally built in a British port, I have to observe that such pretensions are entirely at variance with the principles of international law, and with the decisions of American Courts of the highest authority; and I have only in conclusion to express my hope that you may not be instructed again to put forward claims which Her Majesty's Government cannot admit to be founded on any grounds of law or justice.

I am, &c.
(Signed)   RUSSELL.

No. 15.

Mr. Adams to Earl Russell.—(Received August 18.)

My Lord,   *Legation of the United States, London, September* 17, 1863.

I HAVE had the honour to receive your note of the 14th instant, in reply to mine of the 24th ultimo, presenting the claim of Messrs. Upton on account of the destruction of the ship "Nora." I shall transmit a copy of the same for the consideration of my Government, with whom the withdrawal of instructions necessarily rests. In the meantime I shall abstain from presenting the papers in another case which have come to hand until further advices.

I cannot but regret that your Lordship should have adduced the evidence of Mr. Laird in support of any proposition made to my Government. I trust that I may be pardoned if I remind you that the statements made heretofore by that person in Parliament respecting their action are not such as are likely to lead to their implicit credence in any relating to his own.

I pray, &c.
(Signed)   CHARLES FRANCIS ADAMS.

No. 16.

Mr. Adams to Earl Russell.—(Received September 30.)

My Lord,   *Legation of the United States, London, September* 29, 1863.

I HAVE the honour to transmit the copy of a letter received by me from Mr. Walter Graham, Consul of the United States at Cape Town, in relation to certain occurrences at that place connected with the armed vessel called the "Alabama."

Without intending to sustain all the allegations therein contained, I cannot but consider that a sufficient basis of fact exists to support his remonstrance against the recognition of the captures of vessels, which appears to have been, at least partially, made by the authorities at Cape Town.

In the absence of special instructions on the subject, I take the liberty simply to present the papers for your Lordship's consideration, not doubting the disposition of Her Majesty's Government to do full justice in the premises.

I pray, &c.
(Signed)   CHARLES FRANCIS ADAMS.

Inclosure in No. 16.

Mr. Graham to Mr. Adams.

United States' Consulate, Cape Town, Cape of Good Hope,

Sir,   *August* 17, 1863.

THE Confederate steamer "Alabama" arrived on this coast on the 27th day of July, having captured six American vessels from the time she left Bahia, Brazil, viz., the

* No. 13.

"Amazonian," "Talisman," "Conrad," "S. Gildersleve," "Anna F. Schmidt," and "Express."

On the same day that she arrived on this coast she spoke a small British schooner named the "Rover," which reported her next day at this port (July 28). She was afterwards seen by other vessels on the morning of the 28th, but no intelligence was received here that she had entered any of the ports or bays of this Colony until Tuesday, the 4th of August, when the British schooner "Atlas" reported that she had entered Saldanha Bay on the 28th, and was still there, her crew being engaged in painting her.

Captain Boyce, of the "Atlas," said he was requested by Captain Semmes to take some prisoners to me at Cape Town, but he declined to do so.

On hearing this intelligence I wrote the following letter to the Governor, which I carried in person, to request an interview on the subject to which it treated :—

"*United States' Consulate, Cape Town, August* 4, 1863.
"His Excellency Sir Philip E. Wodehouse.
"Sir,

"From reliable information received by me, and which you are also doubtless in possession of, a war-steamer called the ' Alabama ' is now in Saldanha Bay being painted, discharging prisoners of war, &c.

"The vessel in question was built, in England, to prey upon the commerce of the United States of America, and escaped therefrom while on her trial-trip, forfeiting bonds of 20,000*l.*, which the British Government exacted under the Foreign Enlistment Act.

"Now, as your Government has a Treaty of Amity and Commerce with the United States, and has not recognized the persons in revolt against the United States as a Government at all, the vessel alluded should be at once seized and sent to England, from whence she clandestinely escaped. Assuming that the British Government was sincere in exacting the bonds, you have doubtless been instructed to send her home to England, where she belongs. But if, from some oversight, you have not received such instructions, and you decline the responsibility of making the seizure, I would most respectfully protest against the vessel remaining in any port of the Colony another day. She has been at Saldanha Bay four [six] days already; and a week previously on the coast, and has forfeited all right to remain an hour longer by this breach of neutrality. Painting a ship does not come under the head of ' necessary repairs,' and is no proof that she is unseaworthy ; and to allow her to visit other ports after she has set the Queen's proclamation of neutrality at defiance would not be regarded as in accordance with the spirit and purpose of that document.

"Yours, &c.
(Signed) "WALTER GRAHAM, *United States' Consul.*"

Not finding the Governor at home, I left the above letter. Next morning, the 5th of August, I received the following :—

"Sir, "*Colonial Office, August* 5, 1853.

"I am directed by the Governor to acknowledge the receipt of your letter of yesterday's date relative to the ' Alabama.'

"His Excellency has no instructions, neither has he any authority, to seize or detain that vessel ; and he desires me to acquaint you that he has received a letter from the Commander, dated the 1st instant, stating that repairs were in progress, and as soon as they were completed he intended to go to sea. He further announces his intention of respecting strictly the neutrality of the British Government.

"The course which Captain Semmes here proposes to take is, in the Governor's opinion, in conformity with the instructions he has himself received relative to ships of war and privateers belonging to the United States and the States calling themselves the Confederate States of America visiting British ports.

"The reports received from Saldanha Bay induce the Governor to believe that the vessel will leave that harbour as soon as her repairs are completed ; but he will, immediately on receiving intelligence to the contrary, take the necessary steps for enforcing the observance of the rules laid down by Her Majesty's Government.

"I have, &c.
(Signed) "L. ADAMSON,
"For the Colonial Secretary."

About 2 o'clock P.M. on the same day (August 5), it was reported from the signal-station of the harbour that the steamer "Alabama" was standing in, and also an American barque ; and shortly after it was signalled that the steamer was standing towards the

uc. On hearing this I at once took a cab and proceeded in the direction of Green
t, about two miles from my office, where I witnessed the capture of the barque "Sea
e" by the "Alabama." I immediately proceeded to the Governor's house and told him
; I had seen, protesting at the same time against the capture because it was permitted
ritish waters.

His Excellency remarked that the question of infringement of neutral rights would be
ly dependent on testimony; but he assured me that in any event no breach of
rality would be permitted, so far as he could prevent it. He concluded the interview
:ating that he would immediately telegraph the Admiral of the station at Simon's Bay
nd a war-vessel round to this harbour (Table Bay) to enforce a strict neutrality; and
ested me to put my protest in writing.

At 3 o'clock I returned to my office, and at 4 o'clock I dispatched the following
r :—

"United States' Consulate, Cape Town, August 5, 1863.

his Excellency Sir Philip E. Wodehouse.

"The Confederate steamer 'Alabama' has just captured an American barque off Green
t, or about four miles from the nearest land (Robben Island). I witnessed the capture
my own eyes, as did hundreds of others at the same time. This occurrence at the
.nce of Table Bay, and clearly in British waters, is an insult to England, and a grievous
y to a friendly Power, the United States.

"Towards the Government of my country and her domestic enemies the Government
igland assumes a position of neutrality, and if the neutrality can be infringed with
nity, in this bold and daring manner, the Government of the United States will no
t consider the matter as one requiring immediate explanation.

"Believing that the occurrence was without your knowledge or expectation, and
ig you will take such steps to redress the outrage as the exigency requires,
, &c.

(Signed) "WALTER GRAHAM, United States' Consul."

About 5 o'clock his Excellency sent for me to the Custom-house, and informed me
Captain Semmes desired to land some prisoners, and that he, the Governor, would
; permission provided I would agree tò support them. This I consented to do, and
ȝovernor then acknowledged the receipt of my letter, and repeated his assurances
no breach of neutrality would be permitted.

Next morning (Thursday, August 6), l received the following :—

"Colonial Office, August 6, 1863.

"I am directed by the Governor to acknowledge the receipt of your letter of yester-
date respecting the capture of the 'Sea Bride' by the 'Alabama,' and to acquaint
that he will lose no time in obtaining accurate information as to the circumstances of
:apture.

"I have, &c.
(Signed) "RAWSON W. RAWSON, Colonial Secretary."

About the same time this letter was received all the prisoners were landed, fifteen of
n were the crew of the "Anna F. Schmidt," fifteen of the "Express," and twelve of
'Sea Bride."

On the afternoon of the same day I dispatched the following :—

"United States' Consulate, Cape Town, August 6, 1863.

"I have the honour to acknowledge the receipt of your despatch of this date.

"I beg now to inclose, for your Excellency's perusal, the affidavit of Captain Charles F.
:e, of the 'Sea Bride,' protesting against the capture of the said barque in British
:s. The bearings taken by him at the time of capture conclusively show that she was
:utral waters, being about two and a-half miles from Robben Island. This statement
ibtless more satisfactory than the testimony of persons who measured the distance by
ye.

"I believe there is no law defining the word 'coast' other than international law.
law has always limited neutral waters to the fighting distance from land, which, upon
nvention of gunpowder, was extended to a distance of three nautical miles from land
straight coast, and by the same rule, since the invention of Armstrong rifled cannon, to

" But all waters inclosed by a line drawn between two promontories or headlands are recognized by all nations as neutral, and England was the first that adopted the rule, calling such waters the ' King's chambers.' By referring to ' Wheaton's Digest,' page 234, or any other good work on international law, you will find the above rules laid down and elucidated.

" The fact that the prize has not already been burned, and that her fate is still in suspense, is clear proof that Captain Semmes had misgivings as to the legality of the capture, and awaits your Excellency's assent. If you decide that the prize was legally taken, you will assume a responsibility which Captain Semmes himself declined to take.

" I have, &c.

(Signed) " WALTER GRAHAM, *United States' Consul.*"

"*United States' Consulate, Cape Town, August* 6, 1863.

"ON this 6th day of August, A.D. 1863, personally appeared before me, Walter Graham, Consul of the United States at Cape Town, Charles F. White, Master of the barque ' Sea Bride,' of Boston, from New York, and declared on affidavit that, on the 3rd day of August instant, he sighted Table Mountain and made for Table Bay, but that on the 4th instant, night coming on, he was compelled to stand out. On the 5th instant he again made for the anchorage, and about 2 P M. saw a steamer standing towards the barque, which he supposed was the English mail-steamer, but on nearing her he found her to be the Confederate steamer ' Alabama.' He, Captain White, was peremptorily ordered to heave his vessel to as a prize to the ' Alabama.' One gun was first fired, and immediately after the demand was made another gun was fired. Two boats were lowered from the 'Alabama' and sent on board the barque. The officer in charge of these boats demanded the ship's papers, which the said Master was compelled to take on board the said steamer. This happened about a quarter before 3 o'clock. He and his crew were immediately taken from his vessel and placed as prisoners on board the 'Alabama,' the officers and crew being put in irons. The position of the barque at the time of capture was as follows : Green Point Light-house bearing south by east ; Robben Island Light-house, north-east.

" The said appearer did further protest against the illegal capture of said vessel, as she was in British waters at the time of capture, according to bearings.

" Thus done and protested before me, the said Consul, the day, month, and year above written.

(Signed) " WALTER GRAHAM, *United States' Consul.*
" CHARLES F. WHITE, *Master, ' Sea Bride.'* "

Next morning (August 7) I received the following :—

" Sir, " *Colonial Office, August* 7, 1863.
" I am directed by the Governor to acknowledge the receipt of your letter of yesterday's date, inclosing an affidavit made by the master of the ' Sea Bride,' and to acquaint you that an inquiry into them is now in progress.
" I have, &c.
(Signed) " RAWSON W. RAWSON, *Colonial Secretary.*"

On the same day I sent the Governor the following :—

" *United States' Consulate, Cape Town, August* 7, 1863.
" His Excellency Sir Philip E. Wodehouse.
" Sir,
" Understanding from your letter of this date, received this morning, that the case of the ' Sea Bride ' is still pending, I inclose the affidavits of the first officer of that vessel and the cook and steward, which I hope will throw additional light on the subject.
" From the affidavit of the first officer it appears that the alleged prize was brought with one and a-half miles of Green Point Light-house yesterday, at 1 o'clock P.M. Now, as the vessel was at that time in charge of a prize crew, it was a violation of neutrality as much as if the capture had been made at the same distance from land.
" Pending your decision of the case I would most respectfully suggest that the prize crew on board the ' Sea Bride ' be removed, and that the vessel be put in charge of a crew from Her Majesty's ship ' Valorous.'
(Signed) " WALTER GRAHAM, *United States' Consul.*"

The inclosures of the above letter gave the bearing of the ship at the time mentioned, which were as follows: Robben Island Light-house, north-east by north-½-north; Green Point Light-house, south-west-½-west.

The steward also testified that orders were given to burn the "Sea Bride" at 2 o'clock A.M., on the 6th, which were afterwards countermanded when all was ready.

On Friday I learned, unofficially, that testimony had been taken that day before a Clerk of the Peace in Cape Town, in relation to the capture of the "Sea Bride," and that the testimony consisted of statements as to the distance from land, estimated by persons on land, at the time of capture, and that the testimony of Captain White and others of the "Sea Bride" and of the "Alabama." was thrown out or not taken.

On Saturday at 4 o'clock P.M. I received the following :—

"Sir,   "*Colonial Office, August* 8, 1863.

"With reference to the correspondence that has passed relative to the capture by the Confederate States' steamer 'Alabama' of the barque 'Sea Bride,' I am directed by the Governor to acquaint you that, on the best information he has been able to procure, he has come to the conclusion that the capture cannot be held to be illegal, or in violation of the neutrality of the British Government, by reason of the distance from land at which it took place.

"His Excellency will, by next mail, make a full report of the case to Her Majesty's Government.

"I have, &c.
(Signed)   "RAWSON W. RAWSON, *Colonial Secretary.*"

On Monday morning I dispatched the following :—

                   "*United States' Consulate, Cape Town, August* 10, 1863.
"His Excellency Sir Philip E. Wodehouse.   •
"Sir,
"Your decision in the case of the 'Sea Bride' was duly received at 4 o'clock P.M. on Saturday. In communicating that decision you simply announce that the vessel was, in your opinion, and according to evidence before you, a legal prize to the 'Alabama;' but you omit to state the principle of international law that governed your decision, and neglect to furnish me with the evidence relied upon by you.

"Under these circumstances I can neither have the evidence verified or rebutted here, nor am I enabled to transmit it as it stands to the American Minister at London, nor to the United States' Government at Washington. An invitation to be present when the *ex parte* testimony was taken was not extended to me, and I am therefore ignorant of the tenor of it, and cannot distinguish the portion thrown out from that which was accepted. If your decision is that the neutral waters of this Colony only extend a distance of three miles from land, the character of that decision would have been aptly illustrated to the people of Cape Town had an American war-vessel appeared on the scene, and engaged the 'Alabama' in battle. In such a contest with cannon carrying a distance of six miles (three over land), the crashing buildings in Cape Town would have been an excellent commentary on your decision.

"But the decision has been made and cannot be revoked here, so that further comment at present is, therefore, unnecessary. It can only be reversed by the Government you represent, which it probably will be when the United States' Government shall claim indemnity for the owners of the 'Sea Bride.'

"An armed vessel named the 'Tuscaloosa,' claiming to act under the authority of the so-called Confederate States, entered Simon's Bay on Saturday the 8th instant. That vessel was formerly owned by citizens of the United States, and while engaged in lawful commerce was captured as a prize by the 'Alabama.' She was subsequently fitted out with arms by the 'Alabama' to prey upon the commerce of the United States, and now, without having been condemned as a prize by any Admiralty Court of any recognized Government, she is permitted to enter a neutral port in violation of the Queen's Proclamation, with her original cargo on board. Against this proceeding I hereby most emphatically protest, and I claim that the vessel ought to be given up to her lawful owners. The capture of the 'Sea Bride' in neutral waters together with the case of the 'Tuscaloosa,' also a prize, constitute the latest and best illustration of British neutrality that has yet been given.

                    "I have, &c.
        (Signed)   "WALTER GRAHAM, *United States' Consul.*'

On the same day I received the following :—

"Sir,   "*Colonial Office, August* 10, 1863.

"I am directed by the Governor to acknowledge the receipt of your letter of this date, and to state with reference to that part of it which relates to the 'Tuscaloosa,' that his Excellency is still in correspondence with the Commander-in-chief respecting the character of that vessel, and the privileges to which she is entitled.

"I have, &c.
(Signed)   "RAWSON W. RAWSON, *Colonial Secretary.*"

I did not reply to the foregoing until Wednesday the 12th instant, when I sent the following :—

"Sir,   "*United States' Consulate, Cape Town, August* 12, 1863.

"Upon receiving your last communication to me dated the 10th instant, I deemed it simply a report of progress on one subject treated of in my last letter to your Excellency, and I have therefore waited anxiously for the receipt of another letter from the Colonial Secretary communicating the final result in that case. Failing to receive it, and hearing yesterday P.M. that the 'Tuscaloosa' would proceed to sea from Simon's Bay to-day, I applied for an injunction from the Supreme Court to prevent the vessel sailing before I had an opportunity of showing by witnesses that she is owned in Philadelphia in the United States ; that her true name is 'Conrad ;' that she has never been condemned as a prize by any legally constituted Admiralty Court; and that I am *ex officio* the legal agent of the owners, underwriters, and all others concerned. I have not yet learned the result of that application, and fearing that delay may allow her to escape, I would respectfully urge you to detain her in port until the proper legal steps can be taken.

"I am well aware that your Government has conceded to the so-called Confederate States the rights of belligerents, and is thereby bound to respect Captain Semmes' commission ; but having refused to recognize the 'Confederacy' as a nation, and having excluded his captures from all the ports of the British Empire, the captures necessarily revert to their real owners, and are forfeited by Captain Semmes as soon as they enter a British port.

"Hoping to receive an answer to this and the preceding letter as early as possible, and that you will not construe my persistent course throughout this correspondence on neutral rights as importunate, or any remarks as inopportune, I have, &c.

(Signed)   "WALTER GRAHAM, *United States' Consul.*"

Late on the same day I received the following :—

"Sir,   "*Colonial Office, August* 12, 1863.

"I am directed by the Governor to acknowledge the receipt of your letter of this date, and to acquaint you that it was not until late last evening that his Excellency received from the Naval Commander-in-chief information that the condition of the 'Tuscaloosa' was such as, as his Excellency is advised, to entitle her to be regarded as a vessel of war.

"The Governor is not aware, nor do you refer him to the provisions of international law by which captured vessels, as soon as they enter our neutral ports, revert to their real owners, and are forfeited by their captors. But his Excellency believes that the claims of contending parties to vessels captured can only be determined in the first instance by the Courts of the captor's country.

"The Governor desires me to add that he cannot offer any objection to the tenor of the correspondence which you have addressed to him on this subject, and that he is very sensible of the courtesy you have exhibited under such very peculiar circumstances. He gives you credit for acting on a strict sense of duty to your country.

"I have, &c.
(Signed)   "RAWSON W. RAWSON, *Colonial Secretary.*"

On the 17th instant (Monday) I wrote the following letter :—

"Sir,   "*United States' Consulate, Cape Town, August* 17, 1863.

"I have delayed acknowledging the receipt of your last letter dated the 12th August on account of events transpiring, but which have not yet culminated so as to form the subject of correspondence.

"Your decision that the 'Tuscaloosa' is a 'vessel of war,' and by inference a prize, astonishes me, because I do not see the necessary incompatibility. Four guns were taken from on board the 'Talisman' (also a prize) and put on board the 'Conrad' (' Tusca-loosa '), but that transfer did not change the character of either vessel as a prize, for neither of them could cease to be a prize till it had been condemned in an Admiralty Court of the 'captor's country,' which it is not pretended has been done. The 'Tusca-loosa,' therefore, being a prize, was forbidden to enter Simon's Bay by the Queen's Proclamation, and should have been ordered off at once, but she was not so ordered. Granting that Her Majesty's Proclamation affirmed the right of Captain Semmes as a ' belligerent ' to take and to hold prizes on the high seas, it just as emphatically denied his right to hold them in British ports. Now, if he could not hold them in Simon's Bay, who else could hold them except those whose right to hold them was antecedent to his—that is, the owners ?

"The 'Tuscaloosa' remained in Simon's Bay seven days with her original cargo of skins and wool on board. This cargo, I am informed by those who claim to know, has been purchased by merchants in Cape Town ; and if it should be landed here directly from the prize, or be transferred to other vessels at some secluded harbour on the coast beyond this Colony, and brought from thence here, the infringement of neutrality will be so palpable and flagrant that Her Majesty's Government will probably satisfy the claims of the owners gracefully and at once, and thus remove all cause of complaint. In so doing it will have to disavow and repudiate the acts of its Executive Agents here—a result I have done all in my power to prevent.

" Greater cause of complaint will exist if the cargo of the ' Sea Bride ' is disposed of in the same manner, as I have reason to apprehend it will be when negotiations are concluded ; for being originally captured in neutral waters, the thin guise of neutrality would be utterly torn into shreds by the sale of her cargo here.

"The ' Georgia,' a Confederate war-steamer, arrived at Simon's Bay yesterday, and the ' Florida,' another vessel of the same class, has arrived or is expected hourly at Saldanha Bay, where she may remain a week without your knowledge, as the place is very secluded. The 'Alabama ' remained here in Table Bay nearly four days and at Simon's Bay six days ; and as the ' Tuscaloosa ' was allowed to remain at Simon's Bay seven days, I apprehend that the ' Georgia ' and ' Florida ' will meet with the same or even greater favours. Under such circumstances further protests from me would seem to be unavailing, and I only put the facts upon record for the benefit of my Government and officials possessed of diplomatic functions.

"I have, &c.
(Signed)   "WALTER GRAHAM, *United States' Consul.*"

I have not as yet received any answer to the foregoing letter, and I have little else to communicate beyond what is embraced in my correspondence.

The " Georgia " reports no capture since she left Bahia, Brazil. The " Alabama " and " Tuscaloosa " are cruizing on this coast near Table Bay.

No American war-ships have yet appeared here, but they are anxiously looked for.

Two merchants from this place have gone to Saldanha Bay to buy prize cargoes ; when they return I will watch their proceedings closely.

A company of speculators offered Captain Semmes 4,000l. for the " Sea Bride " and cargo, and he would have taken it, but he wanted a bond that they would not revert to the enemy. They offered me a large bribe if I would give my authority to have them sold here for the benefit of the underwriters, they asking 7,000l. for the ransom ; but I refused to give them any authority to sell. This was before Captain Semmes spoke of the bond.

Should anything else occur in connection with this affair I will let you know as soon as any mail leaves here.

*   *   *   *   *   *

I have, &c.
(Signed)   WALTER GRAHAM, *United States' Consul.*

No. 17.

Earl Russell to Mr. Adams.

Sir,   *Foreign Office, October 2, 1863.*
    I HAVE the honour to acknowledge the receipt of your letter of the 29th ultimo, inclosing copies of communications which have been made to you by the Consul of the United States at Cape Town relative to the proceedings at that place of the steam-vessel

" Alabama," and I beg to inform you that the matter has already been brought to the notice of Her Majesty's Government, and is now under their consideration.

I am, &c.

(Signed)   RUSSELL.

No. 18.

Mr. Adams to Earl Russell. - (*Received October 23.*)

My Lord,   *Legation of the United States, London, October* 23, 1863.

IT may be within your recollection that in the note of the 17th of September which I had the honour to address to you in reply to yours of the 14th of the same month, respecting the claim for the destruction of the ship " Nora," and other claims of the same kind, which I had been instructed to make, I expressed myself desirous to defer to your wishes that they should not be further pressed on the attention of Her Majesty's Government, so far as to be willing to refer the question of the withdrawal of my existing instructions back for the consideration of my Government. I have now the honour to inform your Lordship of the result of that application.

After a careful re-survey of all the facts connected with the outfit and later proceedings of the gun-boat No. 290, now known as the war-steamer " Alabama," I regret to report to you that the Government of the United States finds itself wholly unable to abandon the position heretofore taken on that subject.

The reasons for this conclusion have been so often explained in the correspondence which I have heretofore had the honour to hold with your Lordship touching this case that I shall endeavour to confine myself to a brief recapitulation.

The United States understand that they are at peace with Great Britain. That peace is furthermore secured by Treaties which oblige both parties to refrain and to restrain their subjects from making war against each other.

They greatly regret to be compelled to admit the fact that the vessel known first as the gun-boat No. 290, and now as the " Alabama," is roving over the seas capturing, burning, sinking, and destroying American vessels without lawful authority from any source recognized by international law, and in open defiance of all judicial tribunals established by the common consent of civilized nations as a restraint upon such a piratical mode of warfare.

That this vessel was built with the intent to make war against the United States by British subjects, in a British port, and that she was prepared there to be armed and equipped with a specified armament adapted to her construction for the very purpose she is now pursuing, does not appear to them to admit of dispute.

That this armament and equipment, adapted to this ship and no other, were simultaneously prepared by British subjects in a British port, with the intent to complete her preparation for her career, seems equally clear. Furthermore, it is sufficiently established that when this vessel was ready, and her armament and equipment were equally ready, she was clandestinely sent, by the connivance of her British holders, and the armament and equipment were at the same time clandestinely sent, through the connivance of the same or other British subjects who prepared them, to a common point outside of British waters, and there the armament and equipment of this vessel as a war-ship were completed.

This war-ship thus deriving all its powers to do mischief from British sources, manned by a crew of British subjects enlisted in and proceeding from a British port, then went forth on her work to burn and destroy the property of the people of the United States, in fraud of the laws of Great Britain and in violation of the peace and sovereignty of the United States. From the earliest to the latest day of her career she does not appear to have ever gained any other national character on the ocean than that which belonged to her in her origin.

From a review of all these circumstances essential to a right judgment of the question, the Government of the United States understand that the purpose of the building, armament, equipment and expedition of this vessel, carried with it one single criminal intent running equally through all the portions of this preparation, fully complete and executed when the gun-boat " No. 290 " assumed the name of the " Alabama ; " and that this intent brought the whole transaction in all its several parts here recited, within the lawful jurisdiction of Great Britain, where the main portions of the crime were planned and executed.

Furthermore, the United States are compelled to assume that they gave due and sufficient previous notice to Her Majesty's Government that this criminal enterprise was

rocess of execution, through the agencies herein described, in one
They cannot resist the conclusion that the Government was then
ions and by the law of nations to prevent the execution of it.
romptness and energy required by the emergency, they cannot but
:heme must have been frustrated. The United States are ready·
ct so far as to acknowledge the propriety of detaining this vessel
but they are constrained to object that valuable time was lost in·
:ffort when attempted was too soon abandoned. They cannot
ieir claim for reparation liable to be affected by any circumstances
nere forms of proceeding on the part of Great Britain which are
.vn control.
les of law and these assumptions of fact resting upon the evidence
ructed to say that my Government must continue to insist that
itself responsible for the damages which the peaceful, law-abiding
States sustain by the depredations of the vessel called the

nclusion, however, it is not to be understood that the United States
:ally, or in a spirit of litigation. They desire to maintain amity as
fully comprehend how unavoidably recriprocal grievances must
ergence in the policy of the two countries in regard to the present
nnot but appreciate the difficulties under which Her Majesty's
1g from the pressure of interests and combinations of British
,t upon compromising by their unlawful acts the neutrality which
med and desires to preserve, even to the extent of involving the
ors of a maritime war. For these reasons I am instructed to say,
; themselves unwilling to regard the present hour as the most
1d candid examination by either party of the facts or the principles
: one now in question. Though indulging a firm conviction of the
iition in regard to this and other claims, they declare themselves
:reafter as well as now, to consider in the fullest manner all the
nents which Her Majesty's Government may incline to proffer in
case of an impossibility to arrive at any common conclusion I am
is no fair and equitable form of Conventional arbitrament or
will not be willing to submit.
views, I crave permission to apprize your Lordship that I have
ntinue to present to your notice claims of the character heretofore
·y arise, and to furnish the evidence on which they rest, as is
;, in order to guard against possible ultimate failure of justice from

these instructions I now do myself the honour to transmit the
:he cases heretofore withheld, pending the reception of later

I pray, &c.
(Signed)   CHARLES FRANCIS ADAMS.

.Inclosure 1 in No. 18.

Mr. Weaver to Mr. Seward.

New York, September 5, 1863.
lose a claim against the Government of the United States, together
evidence of ·the claim, for the loss and destruction of the barque
so-called Confederate States' steamer Alabama. And I beg to
/e it filed for such action as may hereafter be taken, in other cases

With utmost respect, &c.
(Signed)   C. P. WEAVER,
Late Master of barque " Union Jack."

Declaration of Charles P. Weaver.

United States of America, Commonwealth of Massachusetts, Suffolk, ss., City of Boston.
BE it known to all whom it doth or may concern, that on this 23rd day of July, A.D. 1863, before me, George Howland Folger, a notary public, duly commissioned and sworn in and for the county aforesaid, personally appeared Charles P. Weaver, of Braintree, in the county of Norfolk, commonwealth of Massachusetths, master mariner, who did on oath declare that he was the owner of twenty sixty-fourth parts of the barque "Union Jack," of Boston, in the commonwealth aforesaid, of the burden of 482$\frac{87}{95}$ tons, and that he was the sole agent for and representing the owners of the other portions of the said barque " Union Jack," as appears by a power of attorney duly executed, a copy of which is herewith annexed, marked A ; that the said barque was owned as follows :—

Charles P. Weaver, twenty sixty-fourths, Benjamin F. Delane two sixty-fourths, Frederick Chandler one sixty-fourth, Charles A. Cousins one sixty-fourth, Elisha H. Ryder two sixty-fourths, Maurice M. Pigott two sixty-fourths, Albert B. Law one sixty-fourth, Wm. H. Hoskins one sixty-fourth, Henry Pigeon four sixty-fourths, of Boston, commonwealth aforesaid ; Norton Pratt, of South Braintree, commonwealth aforesaid, sixteen sixty-fourths ; Luther A. Robie, of Nashua, State of New Hampshire, eight sixty-fourths, Louisa Wilde one sixty-fourth, Howe Averell & Co. one sixty-fourth, and John Atkinson one-sixtcenth, as will be seen by reference to the certificate of the Collector of Customs at Boston of the register of said barque, which is hereto annexed, marked B ; that the said barque " Union Jack," under the command of C. P. Weaver, sailed from the port of New York, on the 28th day of March, A.D. 1863, laden with a general cargo, and bound to the port of Shanghae, China. That the voyage was pursued without injury and nothing worthy of note occurred on board until the 3rd day of May following, when in latitude 9° 40', longitude 32° 30', the said barque was seized and captured by the Confederate steamer " Alabama," and, by the crew of said steamer, the said barque was set on fire and burned and destroyed, together with her cargo and stores ; that on the 12th day of May following the master and crew of said barque were landed at the port of Bahia, when they extended a protest before Thomas F. Wilson, United States' Consul at that port, setting forth a full account of the seizure and destruction of said barque " Union Jack" and her cargo, a certified copy of which is herewith annexed, marked C ; that by this seizure and destruction this appearer and the other appearers and the other owners, whom he represents, have suffered injury and loss to the amount of 48,720 dollars, as follows :—By the destruction of the barque aforesaid 35,000 dollars, as per estimate of E. C. Davis, Esq., Marine Inspector for the Boston Board of Underwriters, certificate of which is herewith annexed, marked D ; and the further sum of 6,000 dollars being the balance due under the charter-party payable in Shanghae, which together with the premium of exchange on Shanghae at this time, making the sum set forth, a copy of which charter-party is herewith annexed, marked E. And this appearer claims for loss of his nautical instruments and personal effects, stores for the use of the crew and belonging to him this appearer, and his expenses of passage and return to the United States, together with loss to himself, in consequence of the breaking up of the voyage, in the sum of 7,720 dollars, as set forth in statement of particulars marked F, making the aforesaid sum of 48,720 dollars.

And now the said appearer Charles P. Weaver, in behalf of himself and the other owners whom he represents, prefers a claim against the Government of the United States of America, holding them responsible for all losses and expenses arising from the seizure, restraint, detainment, and destruction of the vessel aforesaid, this appearer and those he represents holding themselves ready to furnish any additional proof desired in the premises; and the said appearer believes that in equity the Government of the United States of America is bound to indemnify and hold them harmless for all losses, together with interest and expenses in consequence of the seizure herein set forth.

(Signed)   C. P. WEAVER.

In testimony whereof I hereunto set my hand and notarial seal at the city of Boston, this 23rd day of July, A.D. 1863 ; and the said Charles P. Weaver hath in my presence affixed his name, having solemnly sworn to the truth of the foregoing declaration.

(Signeed)   GEORGE H. FOLGER, *Notary Public and Justice of the Peace.*

KNOW all men by these presents, that we, Abiel Gove and Elbridge G. Choate, ɔ-partners under the firm name of Gove and Choate, Otis C. Howe, John Howe, junior, amuel Averill and Edward Johnson, co-partners under the firm name of Howe, Averill, ɪd Co., Benjamin, F. Delano, Henry Pigeon, Frederick Chandler, Charles A. Cousins, lisha H. Ryder, Maurice M. Pigott, Albert B. Lowe, William H. Hoskins, and Louisa 7ilde, all of Boston, in the Commonwealth of Massachusetts, and United States of America; orton Pratt, of South Braintree, in the Commonwealth aforesaid, and Luther A. Robey, ' Nashua, in the State of New Hampshire, and United States of America, being with harles P. Weaver, of Dorchester, in the Commonwealth aforesaid, the sole owners of the merican vessel "Union Jack," hereinafter described in the following proportions, viz. : ɪe said Weaver, twenty sixty-fourths ; the said Pratt, sixteen sixty-fourths ; the said obie, eight sixty-fourths : the said Gove and Choate, co-partners, four sixty-fourths ; the ɪid Pigeon, four sixty-fourths ; the said Delano, Ryder, and Pigott, two sixty-fourths ɪch ; the said Howes, Johnson, and Averill, co-partners, one sixty-fourth, and the said handler, Cousins, Lowe, Hoskins, and Wilde, one sixty-fourth each, have appointed, ɔnstituted, and made, and in our stead and place, put Charles P. Weaver aforesaid to be ɪr true, sufficient, and lawful attorney for us, and in our names and stead, and to his own ɪd our use, to sell and dispose of, at his discretion, the said American vessel "Union ɪck," whereof he, the said Weaver, is now master, her hull and body, with all the masts, ɪils, bowsprits, boats, anchors, cables, furniture, and other appurtenances thereto belonging, ɪd at such price, and upon such terms of payment, as our said attorney may see fit ; ɪd in our names, and in the name of each of us to sign, seal, acknowledge, and deliver all lls of sale, or such other instruments of conveyance as may be necessary or convenient r the due transfer of the title to said vessel and appurtenances, and to receive payment ɪerefor in his own name and our behalf.

.The said vessel "Union Jack" is registered at the port of Boston, in the district of [assachusetts, in the United States of America; has two decks, three masts, an elliptic em, and a figure head. She is a barque, and her length is $130\frac{8}{10}$ feet ; her breadth $3\frac{4}{10}$ feet ; her depth $16\frac{9}{10}$ feet ; and she measures $482\frac{87}{95}$ tons.

Giving, and hereby granting, unto our said attorney full and whole strength, power, ɪd authority in and about the premises, in our names to seal, execute, acknowledge, and ɪliver all necessary deeds and other instruments of conveyance or acquittances, and to ke and use all due means, course, and process in the law for obtaining and recovering l and singular the sum and sums of money, debts, goods, wares, merchandise, effects, ɪd things whatsoever, which shall be due, payable, or in any way coming to us, in or by ɑson of the premises, and of recoveries and receipts thereof; and in our name to make, ɑl, and execute due acquittance and discharge; and for the premises to appear, and the ɪrsons of us the constituents to represent before any Governor, Judges, justices, officers, ɪd ministers of the law whomsoever, in any Court or Courts of Judicature, and there, on ɪr behalf, to answer, defend, and reply unto all actions, causes, matters, and things what-ɪever relative to the premises. Also to submit any matter in dispute in the premises to ·bitration or otherwise ; with full power to make and substitute one or more attorneys ɪder him, our said attorney, and the same again at pleasure to revoke ; and generally to ɪy, do, act, transact, determine, accomplish, and finish all matters and things whatsoever ɪlating to the premises as fully, completely, and effectually, to all intents and purposes as e, the said constituents, if present, ought or might personally, although the matter should ɪquire more special authority than is herein comprised ; we, the said constituents, ratifying, ɪowing, and holding firm and valid all and whatsoever our said attorney or his substitutes ɪall lawfully do, or cause to be done, in and about the premises, by virtue of these ɾesents.

In witness whereof, we, the said constituents, have hereunto set our hands and seals ɪis 7th day of March, A.D. 1863.

(Signed)	Abiel Gove.	(Signed)	Charles A. Cousins.
	Elbridge G. Choate.		Elisha H. Ryder.
	Otis C. Howe.		Maurice M. Pigott.
	John Howe, Jun.		Albert B. Lowe.
	Samuel Averill.		Wm. H. Hoskins.
	Edward Johnson.		Louisa Wilde.
	Benj. F. Delano.		Norton Pratt.
	Henry Pigeon.		Luther A. Robey.
	Fredk. Chandler.		

Her Britannic Majesty's Consulate, States of Massachusetts and Rhode Island.

I, Francis Lousada, Her Britannic Majesty's Consul for the States of Massachusetts and Rhode Island, do hereby certify that the undermentioned parties, viz., Abiel Gove, Elbridge G. Choate, Otis C. Howe, John Howe, junior, Samuel Averill, Edmund Johnson, Benjamin F. Delano, Henry Pigeon, Frederick Chandler, Charles A. Cousins, Elisha H. Ryder, Maurice M. Pigott, Albert B. Lowe, W. H. Hoskins, Louisa Wilde, Norton Pratt, and Luther A. Robey, personally appeared before me this day, and executed the within annexed document, and severally made oath that it was of their own free will, and for the purposes therein set forth.

In testimony whereof I have hereunto set my hand and affixed my seal of office at Boston, this 7th day of March, A.D. 1863.

(Signed) FRANCIS LOUSADA, *Her Britannic Majesty's Consul for Massachusetts and Rhode Island.*

United States of America, Commonwealth of Massachusetts, Suffolk, ss., City of Boston.

I, George H. Folger, a notary public, duly commissioned and sworn in and for the county aforesaid, do certify the foregoing to be a true and exact copy of an original power of attorney now before me.

In testimony whereof I have hereunto set my hand and notarial seal at Boston this 12th day of August, A.D. 1863.

(Signed) GEORGE H. FOLGER, *Notary Public.*

(B.)

Port of Boston and Charleston.

Custom-house, Boston, Collector's Office, June 26, 1863.—I hereby certify that according to the records in this office the barque " Union Jack," of 482⅞⅞ tons, was registered at this office December 16, 1862, and the following were her owners, namely:— Charles P. Weaver twenty-sixty-fourths, Benjamin F. Delano two sixty-fourths, Frederick Chandler one sixty-fourth, Charles A. Cousins one sixty-fourth, Elisha H. Ryder two sixty-fourths, Maurice M. Pigott two sixty-fourths, Albert B. Low one sixty-fourth, William H. Hoskins one sixty-fourth, Henry Pigeon four sixty-fourths, Abiel Gove and Elbridge G. Choate, co-partners, six sixty-fourths, of said Boston ; Norton Pratt, sixteen sixty-fourths, of South Braintree, State of Massachusetts ; Luther A. Robie eight sixty-fourths, of Nashua, State of New Hampshire. And the following transfers have been recorded since the date of the register:—Abiel Gove and Elbridge G. Choate, by bill of sale, one sixty-fourth to Louisa Wilde, December 19, 1862; recorded December 22, 1862. Abiel Gove and Elbridge G. Choate, by bill of sale, one sixty-fourth to Howe Averill and Co., December 19, 1862 ; recorded January 19, 1863. Abiel Gove and Elbridge G. Choate, by bill of sale, one-sixteenth to John Atkenson, March 6, 1863 ; recorded June 27, 1863.

And there is no mortgage or other lien on record against said vessel in this office.

Given under my hand and seal of office this 26th day of June, 1863.

(Signed) J. Z. GOODRICH, *Collector.*

(C.)—*Marine Note of Protest.*

Consulate of the United States of America, Port of Bahia.

On this 12th day of May, A.D. 1863, before me, Thomas F. Wilson, Consul of the United States of America for Bahia and the dependencies thereof, personally appeared C. P. Weaver, master of the ship or vessel called the " Union Jack " of Boston, of the burthen of 483 tons or thereabouts, and declared that on the 28th day of March last past he sailed in and with the said ship from the port of New York, laden with general cargo, and was captured and burned by the privateer " Alabama " on the 3rd day of May, 1863, in latitude 9° 40', longitude 32° 30', and landed in this port by the said privateer " Alabama " on this day, hereby enters this note of protest accordingly to serve and avail him hereafter if found necessary.

(Signed) C. P. WEAVER, *Master.*

Attested :

(Signed) THOS. F. WILSON, *United States' Consul.*

Consulate of the United States of America, Port of Bahia, Brazil, to wit:

By this public instrument of declaration and protest be it known and made manifest unto all to whom these presents shall come or may concern, that on the 12th day of May,

1863, before me, Thomas F. Wilson, Consul of the United States of America for Bahia and the dependencies thereof, personally came and appeared C. P. Weaver, master of the ship or vessel called the "Union Jack" of Boston, of the burden of 483 tons or thereabouts, who duly noted and entered with me, the said Consul, his protest for the uses and purposes hereinafter mentioned, and now, on this day, to wit the day of the date hereof, before me, the said Consul, again comes the said C. P. Weaver, and requires me to extend this protest, and together with the said C. P. Weaver also came George W. Coleman, mate, and George Loring and Alexander Crozier, seamen of and belonging to the said ship, all of whom being by me duly sworn, &c., did severally, voluntarily, freely and solemnly declare, depose and state as follows, that is to say : that these appearers, on the 28th day of March, in their capacities aforesaid, sailed in and with the said vessel from the port of New York, laden with general cargo, and bound to the port of Shanghae ; that the said ship was then tight, staunch, and strong, had her cargo well and sufficiently stowed and secured, had her hatches well caulked and covered, was well and sufficiently manned, victualled and furnished with all things needful and necessary for a vessel in the merchant service, and particularly for the voyage she was about to undertake ; that nothing worthy of note on board occurred until the 3rd day of May, when in latitude 9° 40' and longitude 32° 30', with the wind at east and light at 11·30 A.M.. saw a sail on the port bow, about ten miles distant, bearing down upon us. At 1 P.M. made out that the sail was a steamer, and evidently intent upon boarding us. Kept the vessel off two points and endeavoured to avoid the steamer, but she came up with us rapidly, and about this time displayed the flag of the United States of America, and as soon as we displayed ours she immediately hauled hers down and signalled us to heave-to. It being now quite evident that she was the privateer "Alabama," and that we were entirely in their power, backed the mainyard. Immediately afterwards a boat came alongside, and informed us that we were a prize to the Confederate steamer "Alabama," the steamer setting the so-called Confederate States flag as the boat came alongside of us. After removing a part of our wearing apparel we were ordered on board the steamer, and at about 7 P.M. the barque was set on fire and the steamer hauled by the wind to the eastward, taking one of the barque's boats with her. At 9 P.M. all of the masts were gone and the hull even enveloped in flames. At daylight next morning nothing of the vessel could be seen. On the 12th of May were landed at the port of Bahia. And these said appearers, upon their oaths aforesaid, do further declare and say that during the said voyage they, together with the others of the said ship's company, used their utmost endeavours to preserve the said vessel and cargo from all manner of loss, damage, or injury. Wherefore the said C. P. Weaver, master, hath protested, and by these presents I, the said Consul, at his special instance and request, do publicly and solemnly protest against all and every person whom it doth or may concern, and against the winds and waves and billows of the sea, and against all and every accident, matter, and thing had and met with aforesaid, whereby and by reason whereof the said vessel or cargo already has, or hereafter shall appear to have suffered or sustained damage or injury ; and do declare that all losses, damages, costs, charges, and expenses that have happened to the said vessel or cargo, or to either, are and ought to be borne by those to whom the same by right may appertain, by way of average or otherwise, the same having occurred as before mentioned, and not by or through the insufficiency of the said vessel, her tackle or apparel, or default or neglect of this appearer, his officers, or any of his mariners.

Thus done and protested in the port of Bahia, this 14th day of May, A.D. 1863. In testimony whereof these appearers have hereunto subscribed their names, and I, the said Consul, have granted to the said master this public instrument, under my hand and the seal of this Consulate, to serve and avail him, and all others whom it doth or may concern, as need and occasion may require.

(Signed)   THOS. F. WILSON, *United States' Consul.*
     C. P. WEAVER, *Master.*
     GEO. W. COLEMAN, *Mate.*
     GEORGE C. LORING, *Seaman.*
     ALEXANDER CROSIER, *Seaman.*

I, Thomas F. Wilson, Consul of the United States of America, for Bahia and Dependencies thereof, do hereby certify that the foregoing marine note of protest and extended protest, Nos. 1 and 2, are true and faithful copies of the originals filed in this Consulate, the same having been carefully examined, word for word, and figure for figure.

Given under my hand and the seal of this Consulate this 16th day of May, A.D. 1863.

(Signed)   THOMAS F. WILSON, *United States' Consul.*

                                                F

Suffolk, ss.

I, George H. Folger, a Notary Public, duly commissioned and sworn, do certify the foregoing to be a true and exact copy of an original Consular copy of protest now before me.

In testimony whereof I have hereunto set my hand and notarial seal at Boston, this 23rd day of July, A.D. 1863.

(Signed)　　　GEORGE H. FOLGER, *Notary Public.*

(D.)

Marine Inspection Office, 76, State Street,
Boston, June 27, 1863.

I hereby certify that the barque " Union Jack," of Boston, was built at East Boston ; launched November 1862; 482 tons burthen; was double deck; her frame was New Hampshire white oak, plank oak ; upper deck beams yellow pine ; lower deck beams oak ; had full sets of hacmatrack hanging knees under both decks ; ceiling between decks was yellow pine ; ceiling in the lower hold oak ; was most thoroughly fastened with iron and copper, and through locust trenails ; was in all respects a very superior vessel ; and when she left this port was worth 32,000 dollars ; was sheathed with yellow metal to 11 feet at New York in March 1863, which, together with other additional expenses, at that time amounted to 3,000 dollars, making her full value when captured and destroyed 35,000 dollars.

(Signed)　　　E. C. DAVIS,
Marine Inspector for the Boston Associated Board
of Underwriters.

(E.)

I certify this to be a true copy of original charter-party.
(Signed)　　　GEORGE A. FOLGER.

This charter-party made the 28th day of February, A.D. 18   , between Captain C. P. Weaver, for himself and owners of the barque " Union Jack," of Boston, of the burden of 483 tons, or thereabouts, register measurement, now lying in the harbour of New York, of the first part ; and George A. Patten, of the second part, witnesseth that the said parties of the first part, for and in consideration of the covenants and agreements hereinafter-mentioned, to be kept and performed by the said party of the second part, do covenant and agree to the freighting and chartering of the said vessel unto the said party of the second part for a voyage from New York to Shanghae, China, on the terms following, that is to say :—

1. The said parties of the first part do engage that the said vessel, in and during the said voyage, shall be kept tight, staunch, well fitted, tackled, and provided with every requisite, and with men and provisions necessary for such voyage.

2. The said parties of the first part do further engage that the whole of said vessel (with the exception of the cabin, the deck, and the necessary room for the accommodation of the crew, and the storage of the sails, cable, and provisions) shall be at the sole use and disposal of the said party of the second part during the voyage aforesaid ; and that no goods or merchandize whatever shall be laden on board otherwise than from the said party of the second part, or his agent, without his consent, on pain of forfeiture of the amount of freight agreed upon the same.

3. The said parties of the first part do further engage to take and receive on board the said vessel, during the aforesaid voyage, all such lawful goods and merchandize as the said party of the second part, or his agents, may think proper to ship.

And the second party of the second part, for and in consideration of the covenants and agreements to be kept and performed by the said parties of the first part, does covenant and agree with the said parties of the first part, to charter and hire the said vessel as aforesaid, on the terms following, that is to say :—

1. The said party of the second part does engage to provide and furnish to said vessel good and sufficient cargo for ballast.

2. The said party of the second part does further engage to pay to the said parties of the first part, or their agent, for the charter or freight of the said vessel during the voyage aforesaid, in manner following, that is to say :—

The sum of 3,000 dollars legal tender notes, or their equivalent, on signing bills of lading in New York, free of all commission or brokerages, that is to say, said sum to be net to them; also 3,000 Mexican dollars, less 2½ per cent., free of all commissions or brokerages, that is to say, said sum to be net to them in three days after completion of delivery of cargo in good order, according to bills of lading, bills of lading to be signed without prejudice to charter-party, gross accounts of freight payable in Shanghae by bills of lading, not to be less than 3,000 Mexican dollars, or their equivalent.

It is further agreed between the parties to this instrument that the said party of the second part shall be allowed for the loading and discharging of the vessel, at the respective ports aforesaid, lay days as follows, that is to say, remaining, except Sundays, twenty-five lay days in New York, and ten lay days in Shanghae, unexpired lay days in New York to ensue to benefit of the second part, that is to say, thirty-five remaining, except Sundays, lay days all sound. And in case the vessel is longer detained, the said party of the second part agree to pay to the said party of the first part demurrage at the rate of 35 dollars per day for first five days, and 50 dollars per day, day by day, for every day so detained, provided such detention shall happen by default of the said party of the second part or his agent.

It is also further understood and agreed, that the cargo or cargoes shall be received and delivered alongside of the vessel, within reach of her tackles, or according to the customs at the ports of loading and discharging. It is also further understood and agreed that this charter shall commence when the vessel is ready to receive cargo at the place of lading, and notice thereof is given to the party of the second part or his agent.

To the true performance of all and every of the foregoing covenants and agreements, the said parties of the first part do hereby bind themselves, their heirs, administrators and assigns (especially the said parties of the first part, the said vessel, her freight, tackle, and appurtenances: and the said party of the second part the merchandise to be laden on board) each to the other in the penal sum of 6,000 dollars.

In witness whereof the said parties have hereunto interchangeably set their hands and seals, the day and year above within.

      (Signed)   GEO. A. PATTEN.
               C. P. WEAVER.

Delivered in the presence of,
(Signed)   JAS. HARTUNNIS.

Received on account of this charter-party, as per agreement therein expressed, 5,000 dollars.
  5,000 dollars.   (Signed)   C. P. WEAVER.
New York, March 18, 1863.

Received on account of this charter-party, as per agreement therein expressed, Mr. George A. Patten's draft on Messrs. Bull, Baden and Co. of Shanghae, for the sum of 3,000 Mexican dollars, less 2½ per cent.
  3,000 Mexican dollars, less 2½ per cent.
          (Signed) . C. P. WEAVER.

Lay days in New York, nineteen, leaving sixteen remaining lay days, Sundays excepted, to be used in Shanghae.
       (Signed) .   GEORGE A. PATTEN.
                C. P. WEAVER.

One additional lay day having been used in New York, making twenty lay days in all, leaving fifteen remaining lay days, Sundays excepted, to be used in Shanghae.
       (Signed)   GEORGE A. PATTEN.
                C. P. WEAVER.

United States of America, Commonwealth of Massachusetts, Suffolk, ss.

I, George H. Folger, a Notary Public, duly commissioned and sworn in and for the county aforesaid, certify the foregoing to be a true and exact copy of an original bill of lading now before me.

In testimony whereof I have hereunto set my hand and notarial seal, at Boston, this 23rd day of July, A.D. 1863.
(Signed)   GEORGE H. FOLGER, *Notary Public.*

(F.)

Property on board barque "Union Jack," belonging to Charles P. Weaver, together with expenses incurred, and loss experienced in consequence of the destruction of said barque by the Confederate steamer "Alabama."

				Dols.				Dols.
Nautical instruments	..	..	..	450	25 barrels flour	..	250	
„ books .	..	..	..	100	4,000 lbs. bread	..	190	
„ charts .	..	..	..	125	Small stores	..	385	
Private library .	..	..	..	150			——	1,200
Clothing for self	..	..	..	175	Expenses of passage and other amounts,			
„ ., wife and children	..	..		200	coming home, 45l. and exchange .	..	320	
				——	Loss by breaking up of business and destruc-			
Ship stores :—				1,200	tion of vessel and other property	..	5,000	
15 barrels beef			225				——	
10 „ pork			150				7,720	

(Signed)   C. P. WEAVER.

Boston, July 23, 1863.

United States of America, Commonwealth of Massachusetts, Suffolk, ss.

Before me, George Howland Folger, a Notary Public, duly commissioned and sworn, in and for the county aforesaid, personally appeared Charles P. Weaver, and made solemn oath of the loss of property as set forth in the foregoing statement, and in the manner as set forth in the accompanying declaration.

In testimony whereof I have hereunto set my hand and notarial seal, at Boston, this 23rd day of July, A.D. 1863.

(Signed)   GEORGE A. FOLGER, Notary Public.

Inclosure 3 in No. 18.

Protest of George Hagar.

United States of America, State of New York, City of New York, ss.

TO all people to whom these presents shall come or may concern.

I, Wm. Aug. Walker, a Public Notary, in and for the county of Queen's and State of New York, by Letters-Patent, under the Great Seal of said States, duly commissioned and sworn, residing in the said county of Queen's, and practising in the city of New York and State aforesaid, send greeting :—

Know ye, that on the 17th day of October, in the year of Our Lord 1862, before me appeared George Hagar, Master of the ship called the "Brilliant," of New York, and noted in due form of law with me, the said Notary, this Protest for the uses and purposes hereafter mentioned, and now on this day, to wit, the day of the date hereof, before me the said Notary, at the City of New York aforesaid, again comes the said Hagar, and requires me to extend his Protest, and, together with the said Hagar also comes Hamilton Bingham, first officer, belonging to the aforesaid vessel, all of whom being by me duly sworn on the Holy Evangelists of Almighty God, voluntarily, freely and solemnly do declare and depose us follows ; that is to say, that on the 13th day of September last, he, the said Hagar set sail and departed in and with the said vessel, as master thereof, from New York, having on board the said vessel a cargo of grain, flour, &c., and bound for the port of London ; that the said vessel was then stout, staunch and strong ; had her cargo well and sufficiently stowed and secured ; were well masted, manned, tackled, victualled, apparelled, and appointed, and was in every respect fit for sea and the voyage she was about to undertake.   Got under weigh on the day of the date above mentioned, and in tow of a steamer and in charge of a pilot proceeded to sea.   At 10 A.M. were outside Sandy Hook, discharged the pilot and steam-boat, and made sail, wind north, and cloudy threatening weather. Pursued the voyage from this date with variable winds and weather, making and trimming sail as occasion required, the pumps being properly attended to, the ship's company being engaged in the usual routine of duty, and without any occurrence worthy of especial mention herein, until October 3rd, which day comes in with strong breezes and cloudy weather, wind from the N.E. and squally, at midnight the same, at daylight more moderate, made sail ; a large ship in sight to windward and standing on the same tack as ourselves, about a mile distant.   This ship we afterwards learned to be the "Emily Farnham," of Portsmouth, New Hampshire, bound to Liverpool, from New York.   At 8 A.M. saw a steamer on the weather bow, about five miles distant, heading to the westward.   At 9 A.M. she hoisted the St. George's Cross and fired a gun for the "Emily Farnham" to heave-to, and immediately afterwards hoisted the flag of the so-called Confederate States of America. The ship hove-to, and a boat from the steamer was sent to board her; the steamer then wore round and made all sail in chase of us. During this time we had all sail set and were making every effort to escape. The steamer gained on us, and at 11·30 A.M. she had gained enough to bring us within range. She then fired a gun for us to heave-to. We did so, when she sent a boat aboard of us with two officers and a boat's crew all armed. The boarding officer demanded the surrender of our papers, and claimed us a prize to the Confederate steamer "Alabama," Captain Semmes. Captain Hagar was then ordered to go on board the steamer with all the ship's papers, which he did, and on his arrival there was ordered into the cabin. There, himself and his papers were examined by the Captain of steamer, who decided that the cargo was not on foreign account, because there appeared nothing in the ship's papers to prove it, though this deponent, George Hagar, earnestly protested that it undoubtedly was, and claimed for it protection on that account, but without avail: and he was peremptorily ordered to sign a document naming the owners of the ship and declaring that he had no knowledge of the cargo being on foreign account, after doing which he was ordered on board his vessel to assist with his crew in getting out the ship's boats and such stores and cargo as the Confederate Captain wanted for the use of his steamer: and further orders were given to bring but one bag of clothes for each man of the crew, at the same time saying they were going to burn the ship. Himself and crew being prisoners and under guard, were compelled to do as they were ordered, after which they went alongside the steamer, from whence they were transferred, together with the captains and crews of several vessels previously captured and destroyed by the steamer, to the ship "Emily Farnham," which vessel lay hove-to a few cables' length distant, having been captured as hereinbefore mentioned, and whose captain was at that time on board the steamer undergoing examination with his papers. The result of that examination was that the cargo of the "Emily Farnham" being admitted to be the property of English subjects, that ship and cargo were released from custody. On board the "Emily Farnham" these deponents, together with the balance of the crew, were ordered and compelled to sign a parole under threats of irons and imprisonment if they refused.

During all this time the crew of the "Alabama" were busy plundering the "Brilliant" of everything that time would allow them to carry away. At 6 P.M. the ship "Brilliant" was set on fire, and at 7 o'clock, from the deck of the "Emily Farnham," we saw her enveloped in flames. She continued to burn all night and at daylight we saw another ship near the wreck, no doubt attracted by the light, and the steamer standing for her; a light breeze sprang up and we lost sight of both vessels during the morning. The "Emily Farnham" proceeded on her course towards Liverpool, and on the 6th following spoke the brig "Golden Lead," of Thomaston, Maine, bound from the Island of Jersey to New York, the master of which vessel kindly took these deponents and several others on board his vessel and brought us to New York, where we arrived on the 16th instant; the balance of the "Brilliant's" crew proceeded towards Liverpool, in the "Emily Farnham." And these deponents further state that when ordered by the captain of the Confederate steamer to do the several acts hereinbefore related, they were threatened with irons and imprisonment if they refused to comply. And the said master further says, that as all the damage and injury which already has or may hereafter appear to have happened or occurred to the said vessel or her said cargo has been occasioned solely by the circumstances hereinbefore stated, and cannot and ought not to be attributed to any insufficiency of the said vessel or default of him, this deponent, his officers, or crew, he now requires me, the said notary, to make his protest and this public act thereof that the same may serve and be of full force and value as of right shall appertain.

And therefore the said master doth protest, and I, the said notary, at his special instance and request, do by these presents publicly and solemnly protest against winds, weathers, and seas, and against all and every accident, matter, and thing had and met with us aforesaid, whereby, or by means whereof, the said vessel, or her cargo, already has, or hereafter shall appear to have suffered or sustained damage or injury, for all losses, costs, charges, expenses, damages, and injury which the master, owner, or owners of the said vessel, or the owners, freighters, or shippers of her said cargo, or any other person or persons interested or concerned, and either already have or may hereafter pay, sustain, incur, or be put upon, by or on account of the premises, or for which the insurer or insurers of the said vessel, or her cargo, is or are respectively liable to pay or make contribution or average according to custom, on their respective contracts or obligations; and that no part of such losses and expenses already incurred, or hereafter to be incurred, do fall on him, the said master, his officers, or crew.

Thus done and protested in the city of New York, the 18th day of October, 1862.

36

In testimony whereof, as well the said appearers as I the notary have subscribed these presents, and I have also caused my seal of office to be hereunto affixed the day and year last above written.

(Signed)   GEORGE HAGAR, *Master.*

HAMILTON BINGHAM, *First Mate.*

(Signed)   WM. AUG. WALKER, *Notary Public.*

City and County of New York, ss.

I, William Aug. Walker, a public notary in and for the County of Queens and State of New York, duly commissioned and sworn, and dwelling in said county, do hereby certify the foregoing to be a true and exact copy of an original protest on record in my office in the city of New York.

In testimony whereof I have hereunto set my hand and seal, October 20, 1862.

(Signed)   WM. AUG. WALKER.

MANIFEST and Freight List of American ship "Brilliant," Captain George George Hagar, from New York for London.

No. of Bills of Lading	Marks	No.	Packages	Weight	Measure	Rate of Freight, sterling	Freight (£ s. d.)	Primage (£ s. d.)	Shippers	Consignees	Total Freight (£ s. d.)
1	J.G.	…	37 casks lard oil	…	6,088 gallons	45s. per ton of 252 galls.	54 7 2	2 14 4	Ames Bigland	Order	57 1 6
2	(C)	…	85 barrels of flour	…	…	4s. 6d. per barrel.	19 2 6	0 19 2	Richd. C. Gurney	Ditto	20 1 8
3	L	…	500 ditto ditto	…	…	4s. 6d. per barrel.	112 10 0	5 12 6	Saml. C. Paxton, Sons, & Co.	Ditto	118 2 6
4	(R)H	1/15	25 hogsheads tallow	31,052 lbs.	…	45s. per ton.	31 3 10	1 11 2	Ruprecht and Forstner	Rosing Brothers and Co.	32 15 0
5	(C)	…	200 barrels zinc oxide	48,400 lbs.	…	45s. per ton.	51 6 4	2 11 2	John Jewett and Sons	Lehigh Zinc Company	53 17 6
6	L	…	1,714 bags, containing 4,879 bushels wheat	…	…	14d. per bushel.	284 12 2	14 4 7	Mark Mandeluck and Co.	Order	298 16 9
7	(T)	…	921 do.	…	…	14d. per bushel.	147 17 8	7 7 10	Ditto	Ditto	155 4 11
8	D	…	146 do.	…	…	14d. per bushel.	24 8 8	1 4 5	Ditto	Ditto	25 13 1
9	N	…	2,339 do.	…	…	14d. per bushel.	385 8 11	19 5 5	Kuauth, Nachod, and Kuhne	Wm. Brandts, Sons, and Co.	404 14 4
10	"3" "19"	…	2,293 do.	…	…	14d. per bushel.	383 3 0	19 3 2	Ferdinand F. Dufais	Order	402 6 2
11	(L) (8)	…	43 tierces of beef	…	…	9s. per tierce.	19 7 0	0 19 4	Thos. Lockhardt	Ditto	20 6 4
12	Various	…	30 boxes bacon, and 9 hhds. porkheads 8 tierces middles	22,695 lbs.	…	45s. per ton. 9s. 2d. per ton. 6s. 6d. per ton.	22 15 11 3 12 0 8 4 0	} 1 19 10	Ditto	Ditto	36 11 9
13	(A)	…	26 barrels ditto	…	2,018½ gallons	45s. per ton.	18 0 5	0 18 0	Mason and Wilkie	Ditto	18 18 5
14	(R)H	…	100 ditto flour	…	…	4s. 6d. per barrel.	22 10 0	1 2 6	W. W. Smith and Co.	Ditto	23 12 6
15	(C)	…	796 ditto ditto	…	…	4s. 6d. per barrel.	179 2 0	8 19 1	Nunzinger and Pitzspice	Roderanchi, Sons, and Co.	188 1 1
16	J.M.G.M.C. & M.P.	…	242 bags corn	…	…	50s. per ton.	41 5 0	2 1 3	H. Sautier and Wierum	Edmund Schluser and Co.	43 6 9
17	H	…	2,324 bags containing 6,604 4/7 bshls. wheat	…	…	14½d. per bushel.	399 0 0	19 19 0	Harmony, Nephew, and Co.	Cavan, Lubbock, and Co.	418 19 0
18	(8)	…	2,000 barrels flour	…	…	4s. 6d. per barrel.	450 0 0	22 10 0	Ditto	C. de Municha and Co.	472 10 0
19	(C)	…	4 casks zinc oxide	3,651 lbs.	…	47s. 6d. per ton.	3 17 0	0 4 3	John Jewett and Sons	Lehigh Zinc Co.	4 1 3
20	Order	…	7,000¾ hhd. staves	…	…	70s. per 1,000.	25 4 0	1 5 3	Dutton and Townsend	Order	26 9 3
21	"21"	…	968 bags containing 2,846 bushels wheat	…	…	14½d. per bushel.	171 19 0	8 11 11	H. L. Routh and Sons	Shippers' Order	180 11 0
22	Various	…	1,750 barrels flour	…	…	4s. 6d. per barrel.	393 15 0	19 13 9	A. H. Solomon	J. Brandon & Co.	413 8 9
							3,252 17 0	162 12 8			3,415 9 8

New York, September 10, 1862.

(Signed) FUNCH, MEINKE, & WENDT. (FOR AXEL GODECKE.)

Ship " Brilliant."—Statement of Facts.

Ship sailed from New York, September 13, 1862, bound to London, loaded with flour, grain, &c.

The freight, valued at 18,000 dollars, was insured in the Atlantic Mutual Insurance Company, of New York. On the 3rd day of October the " Brilliant" was captured by the steamer " Alabama," Semmes captain, and burned. The "Alabama," while pursuing the " Brilliant," carried the Confederate flag.

The owners of the freight, on payment of the subscription under the policy, assigned and set over all claims of loss of freight to the Insurance Company.

Claim.

The Atlantic Mutual Insurance Company claim that the English Government should make good to them the damage they have sustained as per above ; for that in violation of international law they, being neutral,- have permitted the " Alabama" to be built and equipped in their ports for one belligerent to be used in cruizing against the commerce of another.

Agreement.

These presents, made and concluded the 22nd day of October, 1862, between J. Atkins and Co., of the first part, and the Atlantic Mutual Insurance Company, of the second part :—

Whereas, by a certain special policy of insurance, No. 5,574, bearing date September 13, 1862, the said party of the second part became the assurers of the said party of the first part, upon the freight, the good ship called the " Brilliant," whereof was master,   New York to London.

And whereas detriment and loss having occurred to the said insured property, by reason of some of the perils in the said policy mentioned or described, the said party of the first part hath ceded and abandoned to the said party of the second part the said insured property, and all the right, title, interest, claim, and demand of   ·   the said party of the first part, of, in, and to the same. And whereas the said party of the second part have accepted the said cession and abandonment, and have, therefore, paid to the said party of the first part the sum of 18,000 dollars, in full satisfaction of the sum by the said policy insured, and of all things in the said policy contained, on the part of the said Company to be performed. Now, therefore, this Indenture witnesseth, that the said party of the first part, in consideration of the said sum of 18,000 dollars, so as aforesaid paid to   by the said party of the second part, the receipt whereof is hereby acknowledged, hath bargained, sold, assigned, transferred, ceded, abandoned, and set over, and by these presents doth bargain, sell, assign, transfer, cede, abandon, and set over, unto the said party of the second part, and their successors and assigns, the afore-said freight, and all the right, title, interest, trust, claim, and demand of the said party of the first part, therein and thereto.

To have and to hold, recover, receive, and take the same freight unto the said party of the second part to the only proper use and benefit of the said party of the second part and their successors, of and from all actions and suits. and causes of actions and suits, promises, agreements, losses, damages, charges, expenses, costs, claims, and demands whatsoever, both at law and in equity, by reason or in virtue of the policy of insurance herein above-mentioned. And the better to enable the said party of the second part to recover and receive the hereby assigned and ceded premises, the said party of the first part hath made, ordained, constituted, and appointed, and by these presents doth make, ordain, constitute, and appoint the said party of the second part, and their successors, the attorneys irrevocable of the said party of the first part, in the name of the said party of the the first part, but to and for the proper use and benefit of the said party of the second part, and their successors and assigns, by all lawful ways and means to ask, demand, sue for, and recover and receive the said freight, and all moneys thence arising ; and all damages of and concerning the same, of and from all and every king, prince, potentate, state, person or persons whatsoever, and for the purposes aforesaid, in the name or on behalf of the said party of the first part, but at the proper costs and charges of the said party of the second part, and their successors and assigns, to appear, prosecute, and plead in all courts and places whatsoever. And all suits, disputes, or differences in any wise respecting the promises to conform and agree, or refer to arbitration, upon such terms and principles, and in such manner and form, as to the said party of the second part, and their successors and assigns, shall appear fit and expedient. And all needful acquittance, discharges, receipts, deeds, and writings touching the premises, in the name, place, and stead of the said party of the first part, from time to time, to make, execute, and deliver, and generally to do and perform all lawful acts, matters, and things whatsoever touching the premises in as full and ample a manner as the said party of the first part, if personally present, might or could do, or as if more special authority were given them. And one or more attorney or attorneys under them, the said party of the second part, for the purposes aforesaid, from time to time, appoint, and at their pleasure revoke.

In witness whereof, the said party of the first part hath to these presents set his hand and seal, and the said party of the second part have also to these presents caused their seal to be affixed, and the same to be subscribed by their President or their Vice-President, and countersigned by their Secretary, on the day and in the year first above written.

(Signed)   J. ATKINS.

Signed and delivered in the presence of,
(Signed)   E. H. Davis.

Mr. Jones to Mr. Seward.

Office of the Atlantic Mutual Insurance Company,
New York, October 1, 1863.

Sir,

I inclose herewith to be filed, proofs of loss in the case of the ship "Brilliant," as follows :—

1. The Protest ;
2. Freight list ;
3. Assignment to this Company of the claim for damages.

I append thereto a short statement of facts, with a brief claim for damages against the British Government.

Should any further proofs be required I shall be happy to furnish them.

Very respectfully, &c.
(Signed)   J. D. JONES, *President.*

United States of America, State of New York, ss.

By this public instrument be it known to all whom the same doth or may in any wise concern, that I, William Aug. Walker, a public notary, in and for the county of Queens, and State of New York, by Letters-Patent under the Great Seal of the said State duly commissioned and sworn, and residing in the county of Queens, do hereby certify that the annexed is a true and correct copy of the original affidavit on file in my office in the city of New York.

In testimony whereof I have subscribed my name, and caused my notarial seal to be affixed, November 8, 1862.

(Signed)   Wm. Aug. Walker, *Notary Public.*

City and County of New York, State of New York, ss.

On the day of the date hereof, before me, William Aug. Walker, a public notary in and for the State of New York, duly and by lawful authority admitted, commissioned, and sworn personally, appeared George Hagar, who being by me duly sworn, deposes and says, that he was master of the ship "Brilliant," of New York, on her late undertaken voyage to London when she was captured by the English or Confederate steamer "Alabama," or "290," and burned, a more particular account of which will be found in his protest extended before William Aug. Walker, notary public, in the city of New York, under date of 18th day of October last past, in which it is stated that this deponent "was peremptorily ordered to sign a document naming the owners of the ship, and declaring that he had no knowledge of the cargo being on foreign account; that though he was compelled to sign this document, he nevertheless called the attention of the master of the steamer to the fact that the ship's bills of lading were endorsed on foreign account," meaning that the cargo belonged to citizens of foreign States, and protested against the destruction of his ship and cargo for that reason, but no notice was taken of it by the master of the steamer, who would not listen to the earnest entreaties of this deponent to spare his ship and cargo; and when this deponent again told the master of the steamer that the bills of lading were endorsed "on foreign account" he replied to this deponent in the following language : "That is the second time you have told me that; do you suppose me to be a d——d fool ?" That the manner of the master of the steamer was overbearing and insolent in the extreme, and it was at great risk of the personal safety, if not of the life of the deponent, that he so strenuously insisted upon his ship and cargo being released. That he did so nevertheless, and was threatened with irons and imprisonment to intimidate him. That when he signed the document to which reference has been made herein, to the effect that he had no knowledge of the cargo being on foreign account, he said at that time to the captain of the steamer that though he had no actual knowledge as to that, but believed it was because such was endorsed on the face of the bills of lading ; and in reply to this the master of the steamer told this deponent that there was no Consular certificate to that effect ; that he wanted none of his suppositions, he wanted facts only.

(Signed)   GEORGE HAGAR.

Sworn to before me, this 8th day of November, 1862. In testimony whereof I have hereunto set my hand and seal.

(Signed)   WM. AUG. WALKER, *Notary Public.*

On the day and year first above written also appeared before me Hamilton Bingham, who being duly sworn, deposes and says, that he was first mate of the aforesaid ship " Brilliant," on the said voyage ; that he has read the contents of the foregoing affidavit of the master, and that the same is true and correct to the best of his knowledge and belief, always excepting such stated conversations as occurred between Captain Hagar and the captain of the Confederate steamer not held in the presence of this deponent.

(Signed)   HAMILTON BINGHAM.

Sworn to before me, November 8, 1863. In testimony whereof I have hereunto set my hand and seal of office.

(Signed)   WM. AUG. WALKER, *Notary Public.*

Messrs. Atkins & Co. to Mr. Seward.

Sir.   *New York, September*   , 1863.

WE respectfully lay before you the inclosed documents :—

1. Our Memorial in relation to the destruction of the ship "Brilliant" by a steamer calling herself " the Confederate States' man-of-war ' Alabama.' "

2. A certified copy of Captain Hagar's marine protest.

3. A certified copy of ship's register.

4. A certified copy of the crew list.

5. Affidavit of Captain Hagar.

These documents prove that the ship was destroyed by fire ; that she is an American ship, and she was sailing according to the laws of the United States.

We respectfully ask that such action may be taken in the premises as shall seem, in your judgment, to recover from Her Britannic Majesty's Government, 75,000 dollars for the loss of our ship, and 3,415*l.* 9*s.* 8*d.* sterling, the amount of freight she had on board, according to the freight list.

We are, &c.
(Signed)   JOSHUA ATKINS & Co.

To the Hon. William H. Seward, Secretary of State, Washington, D. C.

The Memorial of Joshua Atkins and Edwin Atkins, co-partners, merchants, and citizens of the United States, residing in the city of Brooklyn,

Respectfully represents,

That they, together with George Hagar, master mariner, of Boston, Massachusetts, also a citizen of the United States, are sole owners of the late ship " Brilliant," of New York.

That the said ship " Brilliant " being a legally registered American vessel, equipped according to the laws of the United States, sailed from the port of New York on the 13th September, 1862, laden with a cargo consisting of grain, flour, &c., bound to the port f London, in Great Britain.

The said cargo belonged to various shippers, and each bill of lading had endorsed on it " on foreign account," and the Undersigned had no personal interest therein other than the customary lien for the freight thereof.

That on the 3rd October following she had proceeded on her voyage as far as latitude 40° north, longitude 50° 30' west, when she was boarded and declared to be a prize to a vessel calling herself "the Confederate States' man-of-war steamer 'Alabama,'" who immediately took possession of said ship, against the strong and often repeated remonstrances of George Hagar aforesaid, her master on the voyage; and by order of one calling himself the captain of said steamer (Semmes) there were taken from the ship "Brilliant" sundry boats, and such stores and cargo as the so-called captain wanted for the use of his vessel; and the Confederate crew plundered everything that time would allow them to carry away. That Captain Hagar, his officers, and crew were ordered to leave their ship, and were put on board the ship "Emily Farnham," which vessel lay hove-to, a few cables' length from the said steamer "Alabama," a prize to her.

At 6 o'clock P.M. the said ship "Brilliant" was set on fire by order of the said Semmes, and was totally destroyed with all on board.

The ship "Emily Farnham" was released, and proceeded on her course to Liverpool, whither she was bound, but on the 6th October Captain Hagar, his officers, and part of his crew were transferred to another vessel, spoken at sea, bound to this port, and were landed in New York on 16th of same month.

And now we, Joshua Atkins and William Atkins, and on behalf of George Hagar, sole owner of said ship, do enter our solemn protest against the destruction thereof, and do by these presents demand of the Government of Great Britain full reparation for the same, in the sum of 75,000 dollars of the coin of the United States, being the value of said ship, and 3,415l. 9s. 8d. sterling, the amount of freight she had on board at the time of her destruction.

Your Memorialists would further represent that they make and predicate this protest and demand upon the facts therein stated, which can be verified whenever it shall be found necessary so to do. Said vessel calling herself "the Confederate States' man-of-war 'Alabama'" is an English vessel and no other. She was built at the port of Birkenhead, and was allowed to leave British waters, although information as to her character, and the intention to use her as a privateer to prey upon the commerce of the United States, then and now at peace with Great Britain, was lodged with the British Government. That said steamer "Alabama" (then called "the 290"), was allowed to leave said waters upon giving a bond to return, which it was well known was intended to be forfeited. That she did leave the waters of Great Britain the latter part of July 1862, under the protection of the British flag and manned by British subjects. That had the American man-of-war "Tuscarora," or any other legally authorized man-of-war of the United States seized her after leaving said British waters, she would have claimed her British ownership and her flag as her protection. But said steamer was allowed to leave port under the pretence of making a trial trip, and has never been in any port of the so-called Confederate States so as to change her flag, or to be otherwise than a British vessel.

Your Memorialists would further represent that said steamer, after thus fraudulently leaving the port of Great Britain against the Queen's Proclamation of Neutrality, repeatedly visited or came within the jurisdiction of certain British islands in the Atlantic Ocean, when and where it was well known, and patent to the world, that she had destroyed American vessels on the high seas, and instead of being seized and detained by the British Government as they were in duty bound to do, was allowed every facility for obtaining supplies and advice, and to resume her piratical cruise; that no examination was ever made by said British Government through their constituted agents and officers, as to the manning of said steamer by British subjects, or of the prostitution of the British flag, by thus giving protection to the piracies committed under its folds; and that she was and has continued to be, until after the capture of your Memorialist's ship, principally manned by said British subjects.

In view of these matters, and of others which may be made to appear, your Memorialists do now and for ever enter their solemn protest against the British Government and people, as willing parties, negligently calpable in the destruction of their property upon the high seas, and thus in fact violating the Proclamation of the Queen by building and manning said steamer, and then allowing her to continue her depredations.

And they ask, through the Government of the United States, that a proper representation may be made of their loss, that in the end due reparation may be made to them by the said Government of Great Britain, or that the Government of the United States may assume the same as one of the Governmental obligations to protect the rights of their citizens thus wantonly violated.

And as in duty bound will ever pray.

(Signed)   JOSHUA ATKINS.
             EDWIN ATKINS.

No. 19.

Earl Russell to Mr. Adams.

Sir,   *Foreign Office, October* 26, 1863.

I HAVE had the honour to receive your letter of the 23rd instant.

In that letter you inform me that you are instructed to say that the Government of the United States must continue to insist that Great Britain has made itself responsible for the damages which the citizens of the United States sustain by the depredations of the vessel called the "Alabama."

But towards the conclusion of your letter you state that the Government of the United States are not disposed to act dogmatically or in a spirit of litigation ; that they desire to maintain amity as well as peace ; that they fully comprehend how unavoidably reciprocal grievances must spring up from the divergence of the policy of the two countries in regard to the present insurrection. You add further on, that the United States frankly confess themselves unwilling to regard the present hour as the most favourable to a calm and candid examination by either party of the facts or the principles involved in cases like the one now in question.

With this declaration Her Majesty's Government may well be content to await the time when a calm and candid examination of the facts and principles involved in the case of the "Alabama" may, in the opinion of the Government of the United States, usefully be undertaken.

In the mean time, I must request you to believe that the principle contended for by Her Majesty's Government is not that of commissioning, equipping, and manning vessels in our ports to cruize against either of the belligerent parties—a principle which was so justly and unequivocally condemned by the President of the United States in 1793, as recorded by Mr. Jefferson in his letter to Mr. Hammond of the 13th of May of that year.

But the British Government must decline to be responsible for the acts of parties who fit out a seeming merchant-ship, send her to a port or to waters far from the jurisdiction of British Courts, and there commission, equip, and man her as a vessel of war.

Her Majesty's Government fear that if an admitted principle were thus made elastic to suit a particular case, the trade of ship-building, in which our people excel, and which is to great numbers of them a source of honest livelihood, would be seriously embarrassed and impeded. I may add that it appears strange that notwithstanding the large and powerful naval force possessed by the Government of the United States, no efficient measures have been taken by that Government to capture the "Alabama."

On our part I must declare that to perform the duties of neutrality fairly and impartially, and at the same time to maintain the spirit of British law and protect the lawful industry of the Queen's subjects, is the object of Her Majesty's Government, and they trust that the Government of the United States will recognize their earnest desire to preserve, in the difficult circumstances of the present time, the relations of amity between the two nations.

I am, &c.
(Signed)   RUSSELL.

No. 20.

Earl Russell to Mr. Adams.

My Lord,   *Foreign Office, October* 29, 1863.

I ACQUAINTED you, in my letter of the 2nd instant, that the matters connected with the proceedings of the Confederate steamer "Alabama" at the Cape of Good Hope, to which your letter of the 29th September referred, were under the consideration of Her Majesty's Government.

Those matters were—

1. The capture, by the "Alabama," of the United States' vessel "Sea Bride," within, as was alleged, the territorial jurisdiction of Great Britain.

2. The character of the "Alabama" herself.

3. The manner in which the "Tuscaloosa," alleged to be a tender of the "Alabama," was dealt with by the authorities of the Cape.

On these several points I have to state to you—

1. That Her Majesty's Government are satisfied by the concurrent testimony of the Colonial and Naval authorities at the Cape, that at the time of capture the "Sea Bride" was considerably more than three miles distant from the nearest land.

2. That as regards the character of the "Alabama" that vessel is entitled to be treated as a ship of war belonging to a belligerent Power, and that neither the Governor nor any other British authority at the Cape was entitled to exercise any jurisdiction over her.

3. That as regards the "Tuscaloosa," although Her Majesty's Government would have approved the British authorities at the Cape if they had adopted towards that vessel, a course different from that which was adopted, yet the question as to the manner in which a vessel under such circumstances should, according to the tenour of Her Majesty's orders, be dealt with, was one not altogether free from uncertainty. Nevertheless instructions will be sent to the British authorities at the Cape for their guidance in the event of a similar case occurring hereafter, and Her Majesty's Government hope that under those instructions nothing will for the future happen to admit of a question being raised as to Her Majesty's orders having been strictly carried out.

Copies of the reports from the Colonial and Naval authorities on the matters in question will be sent to Her Majesty's Minister at Washington, who will thereby be enabled to give to the Government of the United States any further explanation they may desire to obtain on the subject.

I am, &c.

(Signed)　　RUSSELL.

No. 21.

Mr. Adams to Earl Russell.—(Received November 2.)

My Lord,　　　　　　　　*Legation of the United States, London, October* 31, 1863.

I HAVE the honour to acknowledge the reception of your note of the 29th instant, in reply to my representation of the proceedings of the steamer "Alabama" at the Cape of Good Hope.

Inasmuch as your Lordship intimates that further explanations will be made to my Government through the agency of Her Majesty's Minister at Washington, I shall confine myself to the transmission of a copy of your note.

I pray, &c.

(Signed)　　CHARLES FRANCIS ADAMS.

No. 22.

Mr. Adams to Earl Russell.—(Received November 2.)

My Lord,　　　　　　　　*Legation of the United States, London, October* 31, 1863.

I HAVE the honour to acknowledge the reception of your note of the 26th instant.

The conclusion to which it would seem that both Governments arrive in regard to the disposition to be made of the claims growing out of the depredations of the "Alabama" and other vessels issuing from British ports appears to render further discussion of the merits of the question unnecessary. It is only to preclude the possibility of any inference growing out of an omission to notice it, that I beg permission to make a single remark in connection with your Lordship's observation that "the British Government declines to be responsible for the acts of parties who fit out a seeming merchant-ship." So far as the vessels now complained of are concerned, I think no reasonable doubt can be entertained from the evidence which was obtained before their departure, that they never bore the semblance of merchant-ships, even to Her Majesty's officers who reported upon them.

I now beg permission to lay before Her Majesty's Government a number of memorials and other papers connected with the depredations of the vessel formerly called the "Oreto," and now the "Florida," which I am instructed to request may be disposed of in the manner indicated in my note of the 23rd instant, to which your Lordship's was in answer.

I pray, &c.

(Signed)　　CHARLES FRANCIS ADAMS.

Inclosure 1 in No. 22.

Messrs. Mann & Co. to Mr. Seward.

Dear Sir,   *Boston, September* 24, 1863.
INCLOSED we hand you the Memorial and Protest of the destruction of the ship
"Commonwealth," of New York, by the war-steamer called the "Florida," commanded
by one Maffit; and we ask, through the Government of the United States, that a proper
representation of our loss be made to the Government of Great Britain, and reparation
demanded ; or that the Government of the United States may assume the same as one of
the obligations to protect the rights of citizens thus wantonly violated; and as in duty
bound will ever pray.

Yours, &c.
(Signed)   N. P. MANN & Co.

Inclosure 2 in No. 22.

Memorial.

To the Honourable William H. Seward, Secretary of State, Washington, D.C.

The Memorial of N. P. Mann, N. P. Mann, Junior, and A. J. Mann, of the city of
Boston, Merchants constituting the Mercantile firm of N. P. Mann & Co., owners
of one-fourth of the American ship called the "Commonwealth," of New York,
of the burthen of 1,275 tons,

Respectfully represents,
THAT said ship, being a legally registered American ship, sailed from the port of
New York, on or about the 19th day of March now last past, laden with a cargo of general
merchandize and Government stores, bound for San Francisco, in the State of California,
under the command of George S. McClellan.
That the other three fourth parts of said vessel were owned by citizens of the United
States, and that she was engaged in the performance of her lawful voyage.
That the intended voyage was pursued without any material occurrence until Friday,
the 17th day of April last, when the said ship was about thirty miles south of the Equator,
and in longitude about 30″ west, at which time and place the master of said ship
discovered a steamer steering toward said ship with the American or United States' colours
flying. That said steamer soon overhauled the ship, and sent a boat's crew on board armed
with pistols and cutlasses. That the said boat's crew announced themselves as belonging
to the war-steamer called the "Florida," claiming to sail under the flag of the Confederate
States so-called, commanded by one Maffit.
That the master of the ship was ordered to repair on board the steamer, with all his
papers ; that the officers and crew of the ship were put in irons and transferred to the
pirate steamer ; and that after robbing the ship of many articles, she was set on fire by
the pirate crew and totally consumed.
And now we, the said Nehemiah P. Mann, Nehemiah P. Mann, Jr., and A. J. Mann,
owners of one fourth part part of the said ship "Commonwealth," do enter our solemn
protest against the destruction of said ship; and do, by these presents, demand of the
Government of Great Britain full reparation for the same, in the sum of 22,250 dollars,
being one-fourth of the value of the said vessel, and one-fourth of the value of the
freight pending, and in course of being earned at the time said ship was destroyed, as
hereinbefore set forth.
Your Memorialists would further represent that they predicate and make this protest
and demand upon the facts hereinafter stated, which, according to the best of their
knowledge and belief, can be fully verified whenever it shall be found necessary, to wit :—
The said steamer calling herself the "Confederate war-steamer 'Florida'" is an
English vessel, and no other. She was built in England, and was allowed to leave the
British waters, although information as to her true character, and the intention to use her
as a privateer, to prey upon the commerce of the United States, then and now at peace
with Great Britain, was lodged with the British Government. That she left an English
port under the British flag, and was manned by British subjects. That had any ship of
war of the United States seized her after leaving British waters, she would have claimed
the protection of the British flag, and have escaped under the cloak of British ownership.
That said steamer has not, as your Memorialists believe, at any time actually become the

property of any parties other than those who caused her to be built and fitted out in a British port.

And your Memorialists would further represent that said steamer called the "Florida," after thus fraudulently leaving the ports of Great Britain against the Queen's Proclamation of Neutrality, has repeatedly visited divers ports in the West Indies which are under the jurisdiction of Great Britain; and notwithstanding the facts were well known by the Government officials at such ports, she has not been seized or detained by the British Government, but, on the contrary, has been allowed every facility for obtaining supplies and advice that she might continue her piratical depredations upon American commerce. That no examination has ever been made by the British Government, through their officers or agents, as to the manning of the said steamer by British subjects, or as to the prostitution of the British flag by thus giving protection to piracy under its folds.

In view of these matters, and of others which may be made apparent, your Memorialists do now enter their solemn protest against the British Government and people as willing parties, negligently culpable, in the destruction of their property on the high seas; first violating the Proclamation of the Queen by building and manning said piratical steamer, and then allowing her to continue her depredations after her character was patent to the world.

And your Memorialists ask, through the Government of the United States, that a proper representation of their loss be made to the Government of Great Britain, and reparation demanded; or that the United States may assume the same as one of the obligations to protect the rights of citizens thus wantonly violated.

And as in duty bound will ever pray.
(Signed)   NEHEMIAH P. MANN.
             NEHEMIAH P. MANN, Jun.
             A. J. MANN.

United States of America, Commonwealth of Massachusetts, County of Suffolk, ss.

Be it known to all to whom it doth or may concern, that on the twenty-third day of September, in the year of our Lord 1863, before me, John S. Tyler, a Notary Public and Justice of the Peace, under the seal of the Commonwealth, duly commissioned and sworn at my office, in the city of Boston, personally came Nehemiah Mann, A. J. Mann, and Nehemiah Mann, resident merchants of this city, to me well known, and made before me the foregoing Memorial and Protest, declaring the same to be just and true. Wherefore, at the request of said appearers, I have caused the same to be verified by the oaths of said appearers, and to be entered in my Notarial Records, to serve as occasion may require.

In testimony whereof I have hereunto affixed my official seal on the day of the date above written.
(Signed)   John S. Tyler, *Notary Public and Justice of the Peace.*

Inclosure 3 in No. 22.

Mr. Boyd to Mr. Seward.
Sir,   *Boston, August* 19, 1863.

HEREWITH I inclose depositions taken before John S, Tyler, Esq., Notary Public, of those of the crew of the "Redgauntlet" who returned to this city. You will observe the main body of this deposition is signed by Charles F. Ellis, George Hammond, and William Hennessy; afterwards confirmed by George W. Fuller, whose parents reside in this city; and then again by him and John Baldwin, the carpenter, particularly as to the fact that the "Florida" had the English flag flying until the capture was completed. I deem the testimony of Baldwin important, as it seems he is an English subject, and very naturally had his attention drawn to what was going on under the English colours.

I am advised to-day by Captain Lucas, from Antwerp, August 4, that his protest, made there before the American Consul, will be forwarded within the week. When received I will forward the same to your Department.
Very respectfully,
(Signed)   FRANCIS BOYD.

46

Inclosure 4 in No. 22.

Affidavit of George W. Fuller and John Baldwin.

BE it known to all whom it doth or may concern, that on this 24th day of July, A.D. 1863, personally appeared before me John S. Tyler, a Notary Public, duly commissioned and sworn, George W. Fuller, seaman, and John Baldwin, carpenter, lately belonging to the ship "Redgauntlet," of Boston, burnt by the piratical steamer "Florida." And the hereto annexed affidavit, made by Charles F. Ellis, George Hammond, and William Hennessy, having been carefully read to these appearers, they hereby confirm the same ; and said appearers did further declare that the British flag was flying on board the piratical 'steamer at the time the officers and boats' crew came on board the "Redgauntlet," and remained flying until the officer had announced to Captain Lucas that his ship was a prize. Afterwards the British flag was lowered, and the rebel flag hoisted in its place.

In witness whereof the said appearers have hereto set their names, in presence of me, the said Notary.

(Signed)   GEORGE W. FULLER.
JOHN BALDWIN.

United States of America, Commonwealth of Massachusetts, Suffolk, ss.

On this 24th day of July, A.D. 1863, George W. Fuller and John Baldwin made oath before me that the foregoing affidavit, by them signed, is true.

In testimony whereof I hereunto set my hand and seal of office.

(Signed)   JOHN S. TYLER, *Notary Public.*

I, George W. Fuller, of Boston, on oath declare that I shipped as ordinary seaman on board the ship "Redgauntlet," on her attempted voyage from hence to Hong Kong; that I have read the affidavit of Ellis, Hammond, and Hennessy, who were my shipmates, hereunto annexed, and that I fully confirm the same.

(Signed)   GEO. W. FULLER.

.Suffolk, ss.

Sworn before me, July 18, 1863.

(Signed)   JOHN S. TYLER, *Notary Public.*

Affidavit of Charles F. Ellis, George Hammond, and William Hennessy.

Personally appeared before me the Undersigned, Notary Public, at my office in Boston, Charles F. Ellis, greenhand, George Hammond, steward, William Hennessy, cook, all lately belonging to the ship "Redgauntlet," of Boston, A. H. Lucas, master, and being sworn to declare the truth, and nothing but the truth, did depose and say :—

That they sailed in said ship from Boston on the 22nd day of May now last, bound for Hong Kong, China, having each of them signed shipping articles for the said voyage ; that they proceeded on the voyage without any material occurrences until Sunday the 14th day of June ultimo, when being in latitude 7° 40' north, and longitude 35° 40' west, at about 6 A.M., they discovered a steamer about fifteen miles distant. The "Redgauntlet" kept her course, and the steamer altered her course, and ran down for the ship. She came up and fired a shot across the ship's bow. She had the British flag on her mizen-yard or gaff. The ship was hove-to by order of Captain Lucas, and a boat came on board from the steamer. There was a lieutenant and ten men in the boat ; the men had cutlasses and revolvers. After they got on board the steamer hauled down the English flag and ran up the flag of the so-called Confederate States. The Lieutenant and Captain Lucas went into the cabin, and said Hammond being in the cabin heard the Lieutenant say to Captain Lucas, that he could take such of his things as he could put into a bag. Captain Lucas asked him to take his trunks, and the Lieutenant assented, telling the Captain to hurry. The rebel officers and men told the crew, as soon as they came on board, that they must each one get a bag and put in such things as it would hold to take with them on board the steamer. This was about half-past 8 A.M. All hands left the ship before 11 A.M., and went on board the steamer. As the men went on deck they were ironed, and then left on deck. The steamer's crew, to the number of about twenty men, went on board the ship, and both stood to the northward. They were in company about twelve days, during which the pirate captured and burned the ship "R. R. Hoxie." Deponents saw on board the steamer the crew of the ship "Southern

Cross," which vessel they were told had been destroyed before the "Redgauntlet" was taken. When the steamer used her sails only, the "Redgauntlet" would outsail her. On the 26th of June, being in about 29° north latitude, and 47° west longitude, the pirates all left the "Redgauntlet," after setting her on fire. This was done at about half-past 5 in the afternoon. The steamer laid-by for about an hour, during which the main and mizen masts of the ship were seen to fall, and she was in a sheet of flame fore and aft. The steamer continued to stand to the northward, and next morning the ship could not be seen. On the 27th of June we fell in with a whaling-schooner, called the "Farmer H. Hill," of Province Town, which the steamer captured. At this time she was carrying the United States' flag, and deponents did not see the rebel flag hoisted. At about half-past 10 the rebels had put these deponents, with all but five of the "Redgauntlet's" crew, and many other prisoners, in all fifty-four, on board the schooner, and she steered for Bermuda. Captain Freeman, the master of the schooner, said that he was compelled by the pirates to give a bond to get his vessel released.

On the 4th of July the schooner arrived at Hamilton, Bermuda, where all the fifty-four men were landed.

The deponents remained at Bermuda until the 9th day of July, when they sailed for New York in the brig "Henrietta," having been provided with a passage by the Consul of the United States.

On the 15th instant, deponents arrived at New York, and came thence to Boston by the Fall River route.

Deponents have omitted to state that on the 18th of June the pirate steamer fell in with an Italian brig, which they boarded: said brig was bound for England. Captain Lucas, Mr. Dodge, first mate, Mr. Almy, second mate, and Mr. Brady, third mate, of the "Redgauntlet," were put on board the said brig, with the masters and officers of other captured ships, by the direction of Captain Maffit.

The rebel steamer was the "Florida," and further said deponents say not.

(Signed)   CHARLES F. ELLIS.
GEORGE HAMMOND.
WILLIAM HENNESSY.

Attest:
(Signed)   JOHN S. TYLER.

United States of America, Commonwealth of Massachusetts, Suffolk, ss.

Boston, July 17, 1863.

Then the above-named Charles F. Ellis, George Hammond, and William Hennessy made oath before me that the foregoing affidavit, by them signed, contains nothing but the truth.

In testimony whereof I have caused the same to be recorded in my Official Record Book, and hereunto set my hand and seal of office.

(Signed)   JOHN S. TYLER, *Notary Public and Justice of the Peace.*

Inclosure 5 in No. 22.

Mr. Boyd to Mr. Seward.

Sir,   *Boston, September* 3, 1863.

I HAD the honour of addressing you on the 19th ultimo, inclosing original copy of the Protest taken here of the crew of the ship "Redgauntlet," burnt by the "Florida."

I have now to inclose original copy of Protest made by the Master, A. H. Lucas, and the three officers, before A. W. Crawford, United States' Consul at Antwerp, to which port the officers were taken, as will appear by the document itself.

I should be glad to know if it is necessary or proper, at the present time, for me, as the owner of the ship, to make any more formal claim on the British Government for the capture of said ship under their colours, and by their assistance in every form.

Respectfully, &c.
(Signed)   FRANCIS BOYD.

48

Inclosure 6 in No. 22.

Protest.

Consulate of the United States of America,
Port of Antwerp.

ON this 31st day of July, A.D. 1863, before me, A. W. Crawford, Consul of the United States of America, for Antwerp, and the dependencies thereof, personally appeared A. H. Lucas, master of the ship or vessel called the " Redgauntlet," of Boston, of the burden of 1038 tons or thereabouts ; and declared that on the 23rd day of May last past, he sailed in and with the said ship from the port of Boston, bound for Hong Kong, laden with ice and general cargo, and arrived in the Italian brig " Due Fratelli," of Genoa, the the ship " Redgauntlet " having been captured by a piratical steamer called the Confederate steamer " Florida," hereby enters this note of protest accordingly to serve and avail him hereafter, if found necessary.

(Signed)   A. H. LUCAS, Master.

Attested :
(Signed)   A. W. CRAWFORD, <i>United States' Consul.</i>

I, the Undersigned Consul of the United States of America, for Antwerp and the dependencies thereof, do hereby certify that the foregoing is a true and genuine copy of the note of protest made by the master of the ship " Redgauntlet," having been compared by myself with the original, and found to agree therewith word for word, and figure for figure.

Given under my hand and the seal of this Consulate, this 31st day of July, 1863.
(Signed)   A. W. CRAWFORD, <i>United States' Consul.</i>

Consulate of the United States of America.

Port of Antwerp, to wit :

BY this public instrument of declaration and protest, be it known and made manifest unto all whom these presents shall come or may concern, that on the 31st day of July, 1863, before me, A. W. Crawford, Cousul of the United States of America for Antwerp, and the dependencies thereof, personally came and appeared A. H. Lucas, late master of the ship or vessel called the " Redgauntlet," of Boston, of the burden of 1,038 tons or thereabouts, captured by the so-called Confederate steamer " Florida," laden with ice and general cargo, who duly noted and entered with me, the said Consul, his protest for the uses and purposes hereafter mentioned ; and now on this day, to wit, the day of date hereof, before me, the said Consul, again comes the said A. H. Lucas, and requires me to extend this protest : and together with the said A. H. Lucas, also come R. F. Dodge, 1st officer, Charles E. Almy, 2nd officer, and C. L. Brady, 3rd officer of and belonging to the said ship, all of whom being by me duly sworn, &c., did severally, voluntarily, freely, and solemnly declare, depose, and state as follows, that is to say, that these appearers, on the 22nd day of May, 1863, in their capacities aforesaid, sailed in and with the said ship, from the port of Boston, laden with ice and general cargo, and bound to the port of Hong Kong ; that the said ship was then tight, staunch, strong ; had her cargo well and sufficiently stored and secured ; had her hatches well caulked and covered ; was well and sufficiently manned, victualled, and furnished with all things needful and necessary for a vessel in the merchant service ; and particularly for the voyage she was about to undertake ; that nothing worthy of note occurred until Sunday, the 14th of June, when in latitude about 8° 30′ north, and longitude 34° 40′ west, at 6 A.M. on that day, the wind being east, discovered a vessel, apparently a barque, two points off the lee-bow, and standing on the wind to the northward ; a ship in sight to windward at the same time also standing to the northward ; shortly afterwards discovered that the barque-rigged vessel was a screw steamer, with two smoke stacks ; at 7 A.M. the steamer bore due west from us, when the British flag was hoisted on board of her ; we set the American flag in answer, and kept it flying about ten minutes, then hauled it down ; at 7·30 A.M. the steamer tacked ship, took in all sail and steamed up towards us ; shortly afterwards a shot was fired from the said steamer towards us, passing a few yards leeward of the ship ; we then brought the ship to the wind in the usual manner, the steamer approached within a few yards to windward and some person hailed the ship, in the usual manner, asking where we were from, and where bound. We replied in the usual manner, and some person on board the steamer said they would send a boat aboard. A boat filled with armed men came alongside the ship, and an officer who had charge of the boat came aboard and demanded the ship's papers to look at ; the moment the officer stepped on board the British flag was hauled down and a flag called a Confederate States' flag (with three horizontal stripes, red, white, and red, with a blue union containing thirteen white stars) was substituted. I produced the ship's papers, and after he had examined them he told me the ship was a prize to the Confederate States' steamer "Florida," Captain Maffitt. I said to the officer that the cargo of the ship was principally British, and directed his attention to the British Consul's certificates attached to each bill of lading. He said that was no protection, that the ship was a good prize, and that I must get ready to go on board the "Florida," adding at the same time that the boat was ready. I asked for the ship's papers, and he said that he would keep them and send them on board the "Florida." I handed him a letter given me in Boston containing invoices and proofs of the nationality of the cargo, but no notice was taken of it. I was told to take nothing but wearing apparel, and not too much of that, as it would not be allowed. He demanded all private arms and pistols, took the two chronometers and all the nautical instruments, and before I had time to pack up any of my clothing two armed men entered the cabin and told me to go in the boat, the officer saying he would send my clothing aboard. I obeyed, as resistance was useless. I, with the officers and crew, was transported to the steamer; on arrival there all, except the first officer and myself, were put in irons. I inquired for the Commander, and asked him if he was Captain Maffitt. He replied that he was, I told him the ship's cargo was principally British, and that the bills of lading had British Consul's certificates attached. He said that made no difference. I protested against his proceeding. He said the ship was a good prize. I asked him if he would bond the ship. He replied, "No ; I shall bond no more American ships ; it is a preposterous idea to think of bonding an American ship in order to save a little British cargo, for since Lincoln has declared the bonds of the 'Ariel' null and void I shall destroy and not bond any American ships I may capture." A prize crew was put on board the "Redgauntlet," and she kept company with the steamer, standing north-north-west. The ship was plundered from day to day, in moderate weather the cargo and stores being transported to the steamer, as well as my own personal property, consisting of a chronometer, a sextant, a spy-glass, an opera-glass, barometer, books, charts, wearing apparel, and other personal property, being appropriated to the use of the steamer, the captain, officers, and crew.

Thursday, June 18, gave chase to and came up with the brig "Due Fratelli," of Genoa. The brig was boarded under the British flag, and on the return of the boat the so-called Confederate States' flag was substituted. On the return of the boat I was ordered to go in the boat with my officers; we obeyed, and were transferred to the brig, without being consulted or having any voice in the matter. The latitude was 13° 27′ north, longitude 40° west, the "Redgauntlet" in company.

Friday, June 19, at 2 P.M., saw the "Florida" and "Redgauntlet" both standing to the north-north-west.

Now, therefore, be it known to whom it may concern, that I, Augustus H. Lucas, late master of the ship "Redgauntlet," of Boston, for and in behalf of all parties concerned or interested in the said ship "Redgauntlet," her cargo, stores, outfits, freight, insurance, or in any other way or manner interested in anything appertaining to said ship, do hereby protest against the capture and piratical detention of said ship and cargo; against the commander, officers, and crew of the said steamer "Florida," collectively and individually ; also against the builders and owners of said steamer ; against the Government or Governments, or belligerents, recognized or otherwise, who may be interested in said steamer ; and against any and all Governments and authorities, local or otherwise, who have permitted the said steamer to be fitted out, armed, equipped, manned, supplied, recruited, or allowed to enter or depart from their ports or dependencies ; and also other persons assisting in the same : and in behalf of all concerned shall hold each and all of them responsible for all damage or damages which may or shall arise in consequence of said capture ; and also for all losses which may occur to the owner or owners, charterers, agents, shippers, consignees, underwriters, master, officers, or crew of said ship, in consequence of said capture. And I, together with the officers of said ship "Redgauntlet," do hereby conjointly sign this protest.

Thus done and protested in the port of Antwerp, this 1st day of August, in the year of our Lord 1863.

In testimony whereof these appearers have hereunto subscribed their names ; and I, the said Consul, have granted to the said master this public instrument under my hand and the seal of this Consulate, to serve and avail him and all others whom it doth or may concern, as need and occasion may require.

(Signed)   A. W. CRAWFORD, *United States' Consul.*
             A. H. LUCAS, *Master.*
             R. T. DODGE, *First Officer.*
             CHARLES E. ALMY, *Second Officer.*
             C. L. BRADY, *Third Officer.*

50

I, the Undersigned, Consul of the United States for Antwerp and the dependencies thereof, do hereby certify that the foregoing is a true and genuine copy of the protest made by the master of the ship "Redgauntlet," having been compared by myself with the original and found to agree therewith, word for word and figure for figure.

Given under my hand and the seal of this Consulate, this 1st day of August, 1863.

(Signed)   A. W. CRAWFORD, *United States' Consul.*

British Consulate, Antwerp.

I, the Undersigned, Her Britannic Majesty's Consul at Antwerp, hereby certify that A. W. Crawford, Esq., whose signature is attached to the foregoing document, is the Consul of the United States residing at this port.

In testimony whereof I have hereunto set my hand and affixed my seal of office, this 5th day of August, 1863.

(Signed)   G. A. GEATTON.

No. 23.

Earl Russell to Mr. Adams.

Sir,   *Foreign Office, November 10, 1863.*

I HAVE the honour to acknowledge the receipt of your note of the 31st ultimo, inclosing further papers respecting the proceedings of the "Alabama" and the "Florida."

I am, &c.

(Signed)   RUSSELL.

No. 24.

Mr. Adams to Earl Russell.—(Received November 14.)

My Lord,   *Legation of the United States, London, November 14, 1863.*

I HAVE the honour to transmit a printed copy of the private journal of an officer of the steamer "Alabama," which seems to have been furnished by the author for publication in the "South African Advertiser and Mail," at Cape Town, in which newspaper it first appeared on the 19th of September last. The author appears to be Mr. G. S. Fullam, a British subject, belonging to Hull. I beg permission to call your Lordship's attention to the remarkable manner in which the narrative corroborates the essential portions of the deposition of C. R. Yonge, heretofore submitted to your consideration, some attempts to invalidate which were made in the course of the trial of the "Alexandra." It likewise confirms, in almost every particular, the correctness of the representations which I had the honour to furnish from the Consul of the United States at Liverpool, of the mode in which the gun-boat "290" was originally equipped, fitted out, and armed from that port.

I likewise pray your Lordship's attention to the abuse shown to be continually made of the national character of this vessel, in the fraudulent assumption of the flag or of the name of any other nation at pleasure, whilst on the high seas. I need scarcely say that such a license to cover piratical depredation has only been obtained for her by the recognition given to the parties in America, authorizing it as a belligerent abiding by the established rules of legitimate warfare.

I pray, &c.

(Signed)   CHARLES FRANCIS ADAMS.

No. 25.

Earl Russell to Mr. Adams.

Sir,   *Foreign Office, November 16, 1863.*

I HAVE the honour to acknowledge the receipt of your letter of the 14th instant and its inclosure, respecting the proceedings of the "Alabama."

I am, &c.

(Signed)   RUSSELL.

No. 26.

Mr. Adams to Earl Russell.—(Received January 13.)

My Lord,   *Legation of the United States, London, January* 13, 1864.

I PRAY your attention to copies of a letter of the Consul of the United States at Liverpool, and of three depositions, all going cumulatively to prove the manner in which the neutrality of Her Majesty's realm has been abused by some of her subjects, for the purpose of carrying on war against the United States. I have every reason to suppose that these proceedings are continued without material diminution.

Renewing, &c.
(Signed)   CHARLES FRANCIS ADAMS.

Inclosure 1 in No. 26.

Mr. Dudley to Mr. Adams.

Sir,   *United States' Consulate, Liverpool, January* 11, 1864.

I BEG to call your attention to copies of three affidavits: one of John Latham, another of his wife, Martha Latham, and the other that of Thomas Wistinley, inclosed. It is a well-known fact that the steamer "Alabama," which was built and fitted out at this port, and manned by British seamen, regularly receives her coal and supplies from this country, and that the families of the men now serving on board are paid once a-month here in Liverpool by M. G. Klingender and Co., and Fraser, Trenholm, and Co., the one-half part of the wages earned by the men on board this vessel. John Latham, of Swansea, in Wales, was one of the men who enlisted on said steamer. During the time of his service on board, his wife, Martha Latham, received regularly each month the one-half part of his wages, which was sent to her by M. G. Klingender and Co., No. 22, Water-street, Liverpool. The money was transmitted in post-office orders. The letters in which this money was sent are annexed to her affidavit, and copies inclosed to you. At the time of enlisting Mr. Latham received a bounty. He sent 5l. of this to his wife by Captain James D. Bullock. This 5l. was paid to Thomas Winstinley for her at Fraser, Trenholm, and Co.'s office by their cashier.

I regard these affidavits as important to show the character and nationality (if she has any) of this vessel, which, built in England, fitted out in England, armed with English guns, and manned by English seamen; supplied with coal and other necessaries while cruizing from England, in English vessels, by English merchants; and the wages earned by the men while serving on board paid here in Liverpool by these same merchants to their wives and families residing here,—stamps her, it seems to me, if anything can, as an English piratical craft.

I am, &c.
(Signed)   THOMAS H. DUDLEY.

Inclosure 2 in No. 26.

Affidavit of John Latham.

I, John Latham, of 36, Jasper-street, Liverpool, in the county of Lancaster, engineer, make oath, and say as follows :—

1. About the 8th or 10th of August, 1862, I signed articles at the Sailors' Home, Liverpool, to ship in the steam-ship "Bahama," Captain Tessier, for a voyage to Nassau and back. The "Bahama" went out of the Bramley Moore dock the same night about 12 o'clock, and went into the river and lay-to. Captain Semmes, Captain James D. Bullock, and some other officers came on board, and about half past 7 o'clock A.M. a tug-boat came alongside with some seamen on board ; the tug-boat accompanied us out about ten miles. The tug then left us, and a tall gentleman, with a reddish face and pock-marked, who came from Cunard Wilson and Co.'s office, left us and went into the tug ; as he left us, he said "I hope you will make a good thing of it, and that you will stop where you are going to." We then proceeded on our voyage, and stood out some days, when we found we were going to the Western Isles.

2. About the 17th or 18th of August we arrived at Terceira, and we there found the

" Alabama" and the barque " Agrippina." Captain Butcher, who was on board the " Alabama." hailed us and told us to go round the island, and he would be after us, but it would take them three-quarters of an hour to get his steam up. We went on, and he followed us, and the " Alabama" went under the lee of the island, and a shot was fired across the " Bahama's " bows from a battery on shore, so we stopped out until the morning. In the morning we went alongside the " Alabama," and some small cases and a safe containing money was passed into the " Alabama" from our ship, and we then parted and anchored a little distance from her, and the barque " Agrippina " went and discharged the remainder of her cargo into the " Alabama." During this time Captain Semmes and Captain Bullock were going backwards and forward to the " Alabama," but would not let any of the officers go. On Sunday, the 24th of August, Captain Semmes came on board the " Bahama," and called us under the bridge, he himself and the officers standing on the bridge ; he addressed us and said, " Now, my lads, there is the ship " (pointing to the " Alabama ") ; " she is as fine a vessel as ever floated ; there is a chance which seldom offers itself to a British seaman, that is, to make a little money. I am not going to put you alongside of a frigate at first ; but after I have got you drilled a little, I will give you a nice little fight.". He said, " There is only six ships that I am afraid of in the United States' navy." He said, " We are going to burn, sink, and destroy the commerce of the United States; your prize-money will be divided proportionately according to each man's rank, something similar to the English navy." Some of the men objected, being Naval Reserve men. Captain Semmes said, " Never mind that, I will make that all that right ; I will put you in English ports where you can get your book signed every three months." He then said, " There is Mr. Kell on the deck, and all those who are desirous of going with me let them go aft, and give Mr. Kell their names." A great many went aft, but some refused. A boat came from the " Alabama," and those who had agreed to go went on board. Captain Semmes and the officers went on board. Mr. Low, the Fourth Lieutenant, then appeared in uniform, and he came on board the " Bahama," endeavouring to induce the men to come forward and join, and he succeeded in getting the best part of us. I was one who went at the last minute. When I got on board the " Alabama " I found a great number of men that had gone on board of her from Liverpool. Captain Semmes then addressed us on board the " Alabama," and Captain Butcher was there also, who had taken the vessel out. Captain Semmes said he hoped we all should content ourselves and be comfortable one amongst another ; but any of you that thinks he cannot stand to his gun I don't want. He then called the purser, and such as agreed to serve signed articles on the companion-hatch, and on signing the men received either two months' pay in advance, or one month's wages and a half-pay note. I took a month's wages and a half-pay note for 3l. 10s. a-month in favour of my wife Martha Latham, 19, Wellington-street, Swansea ; the note was drawn on Fraser Trenholm and Co., of Liverpool, but it was paid at Mr. Klingender's in Liverpool : the note was signed by Captain Semmes, Yonge, who was the Paymaster, and Smith, the Captain's clerk. I sent 5l. and this half-pay note ashore by Captain Bullock, and he forwarded it with a letter to my wife.

3. Captain Bullock on the passage out, and after we arrived at Terceira, used arguments to induce us to join the " Alabama." On several occasions he advised us, and urged the men to join.

4. As soon as the men who had consented to go had all signed articles, the English ensign which the " Alabama" had been flying was pulled down, and the Confederate flag hoisted, and a gun was fired. The men who declined joining left the ship, with Captains Bullock and Butcher, for the " Bahama," and we proceeded, under the command of Captain Semmes ; and I have in the Schedule hereto annexed given a list of the officers and men, with their places of residence.

5. We proceeded on our voyage, and cruised about the Western Isles for some days, and on the following Sunday we fell in with a whaler, and burnt her ; and we then cruized about, and in about two days we fell in with the schooner " Starlight," from Boston. We fired at her four times. Her captain said, " If I had but one gun on board I would fight you." He tried to make the land, but we overhauled him, and he brought-to. We kept the crew of the schooner, and on the next day we landed them at the Western Isles, and took the schooner in tow, for the purpose of decoying other vessels with the stars and stripes. We succeeded in capturing several ; amongst other vessels we captured the " Manchester," of Philadelphia line of packets, bound from New York to Liverpool. We burnt this vessel, having first taken her crew, and we put them on board the " Tonawanda," which we had previously captured, and had then in tow. Amongst the crew there was a man of the name of George Forrest, who one of the Midshipmen recognized as having been a seaman on board the " Sumter," and had deserted. He was brought on board to Captain Semmes, who told him that if he behaved well he should have his pay and prize-money as the

as the other men, but that he had a right to detain him throughout the war without paying him a cent. Forrest was retained on board the "Alabama," was frequently punished by having his hands and legs fastened to the rigging, the punishment being known as the "spread eagle," and he would be kept in this position for four hours at a time, and this was done at least twenty times, and at last they ironed his legs and arms, and sent him on shore on a desolate island called Blencoola some 200 miles from the mainland, and left him. The crew subscribed some 17*l*., unknown to Captain Semmes, which we gave him in the hope of its being some inducement to a vessel to take him off.

6. The barque "Agrippina," flying the British flag, and loaded with coals from Cardiff, was at Martinique when we arrived there; and she went out to sea, and whilst out she supplied us with coal. After this we went to Arkaskees, where we stopped and painted the ship, and then went towards Galveston, and off that place we fell in with the American ship "Hatteras," which we sunk. We got her crew on board, and proceeded to Port Royal, Jamaica. There I ran away, and left the "Alabama." Whilst there the "Alabama" enlisted two British sailors, who had deserted from Her Majesty's ships "Jason" and "Steady." Thomas Potter, who was fireman, also ran away, but the men of the "Alabama" came after him and arrested him, and took him back to the ship. Clarence Yonge, the purser, also left the ship. I was also arrested at an hotel in Jamaica by the "Alabama's" crew. They wanted to force me on board, but I refused to go until I had seen the Governor of the island, whose residence was some fifteen miles' distance; and I saw the Superintendent of Police, who on my producing a certificate that I was a Naval Coast Volunteer on board Her Majesty's ship "Majestic," I was released.

7. My wife received my half-pay. She used to receive it by Post-office order, payable at Swansea; and to obtain this she every month used to write Messrs. Fraser, Trenholm, and Co., or M. G. Klingender and Co., Liverpool, inclosing the half-pay note, and the latter firm used to send her a Post-office order for the 3*l*. 9*s*. 5*d*., deducting the cost of the order and the postage. In February or March she wrote as usual for the half-pay note. They wrote in reply that they could send her no more money, as I had left the ship, but they did not return her the half-pay note.

8. On my return I called at Fraser, Trenholm, and Co.'s office for the balance of my wages, but they declined to pay me, and denied all knowledge of the ship; but Mr. Cooper gave me the name of Mr. M. G. Klingender, and told me to see him, and see if he could arrange it. I did so, but he told me he would not do so, as they had received a note from Captain Semmes that I had deserted at Jamaica.

9. The guns comprising the armament on the "Alabama" have Fawcett, Preston, and Co.'s marks on them, showing they were made by this firm.   ●
        (Signed)   JOHN LATHAM.

Sworn and subscribed to before me this 8th day of January, 1864, at Liverpool, in the county of Lancaster.
      (Signed)   J. PEARSON, *a Commissioner to administer Oaths in Chancery in England.*

SCHEDULE before referred to.

Officers and Crew of the steamer "Alabama."

Raphael Semmes, Commander.
J. M. Kell, First Lieutenant.
Richard F. Armstrong, Second Lieutenant.
Joseph Wilson, Third Lieutenant.
John Low, Fourth Lieutenant, Englishman.
Arthur Sinclair, Master, that is Sailing Master.
Francis L. Galt, Surgeon, from Virginia, now acting as Paymaster.
Miles J. Freeman, First Assistant Engineer, ranks as Chief, born in Wales, does not know whether naturalized.
David Herbert Llewellyn, Assistant Surgeon, Englishman.

B. K. Howell, brother-in-law of Jeff. Davis, Lieutenant of Marines (no Marines on board).
Wm. H. Sinclair, Midshipman.
Irvine S. Bullock, Midshipman, Captain Bullock's brother.
Eugene Maffitt, Midshipman, Captain Maffitt's son.
Edward Maffitt Anderson, Midshipman, son of Colonel Anderson.
Wm. P. Brooks, Second Assistant Engineer.
S. N. Cummings, Third Assistant Engineer.
Matthew O'Brien, Third Assistant Engineer.

John M. Pundt, Third Assistant Engineer.

George T. Fullam, First Master's Mate, Englishman.

James Evans, Second Master's Mate, Charleston Pilot.

W. B. Smith, Captain's Clerk.

Benjamin L. McCaskey, Boatswain.

T. O. Cuddy, Gunner.

Wm. Robinson, Carpenter.

Henry Allcott, Sailmaker, Englishman.

Clarence R. Yonge, Paymaster.

Petty Officers and Seamen.

James King, Master-at-arms, Savannah Pilot.

Adolphus Marmelegs, Portuguese.

Wm. A. King, Quartermaster.

James King, Master-at-arms.

James G. Dent, Quartermaster.

Wm. Forestall, Quartermaster, Englishman.

Ralph Masters, Quarter Gunner, Irishman.

Wm. Crawford, Englishman, lives in Liverpool, belongs to Royal Naval Reserve.

George Addison, Englishman, lives in Liverpool.

Wm. Brinton, Englishman, Royal Naval Reserve.

— Robinson, Head Carpenter.

George Harwood, Boatswain's Mate, Englishman, Pensioner from English Navy, joined her at Liverpool Home, now is in " Southerner" as Boatswain, lives in Liverpool.

Michael Kinshler, Irishman, Fireman, has a pension in England.

Brent Johnson, Second Boatswain's Mate, Englishman, Naval Reserve man, joined vessel at Liverpool.

Wm. Purdy, Sailmaker's Mate, Irishman by birth, lives in Liverpool, belongs to Naval Reserves, joined her in Liverpool.

John Latham, Fireman, an Englishman, belongs to Coast Volunteers, enlisted in " Alabama" at Terceira.

David Roach, Fireman, Englishman, resides in Liverpool, belongs to Royal Naval Reserve; enlisted in Liverpool; left her 22nd November.

Thomas Murphy, Fireman, Englishman, left her at Western Islands.

Thomas Welch, Englishman, left the ship; he enlisted in the " Alabama" in Liverpool.

James Smith, Captain of Forecastle, Englishman, residing in Liverpool, belongs to Naval Reserve; enlisted on board of " Alabama" in Liverpool.

Edward Fitzmorris, Englishman, enlisted on " Alabama" in Liverpool, is at home now; his wife lives at Aigburth.

George Addison, Fireman, Englishman, lives at Liverpool, Copperas Hill; enlisted at Terceira.

James McFadgeon, Fireman, Englishman, lives at No. 6, West Derby-street, Liverpool; enlisted at Terceira, is now at home.

Thomas Potter, Fireman, Englishman, enlisted in " Alabama" at Liverpool, lives in Athol-street, Liverpool, deserted at Jamaica; they arrested him there and carried him on board; his wife lives in Liverpool now.

Samuel Williams, Fireman, lives in Liverpool, born in Wales, enlisted in " Alabama" at Liverpool.

Patrick Bradley, Fireman, Englishman, resides in Liverpool, enlisted in Liverpool.

John Orrigin, Fireman, Irishman, resides in Athol-street, Liverpool, enlisted in Liverpool.

Orran Duffy, Fireman, Irishman.

Peter Duncan, Fireman, Englishman, resides in Liverpool, enlisted in Liverpool.

Wm. Nevins, Coal-passer, Englishman, belongs to Naval Reserve, enlisted at Liverpool.

Andrew Shillings, Scotchman, resides in Athol-street, Liverpool; has a wife; enlisted at Liverpool, is a Fireman.

Charles Priest, Coal-passer, is a German.

George Yeoman, Ordinary Seaman, Englishman, enlisted at Terceira.

George Freemantle, Seaman, Englishman, enlisted at Terceira.

Frederick Johns, Purser's Steward, Englishman, resides in Liverpool; father keeps a coal-yard in Howard-street; enlisted at Terceira.

John Grandy, boy, English, lives in Liverpool.

Thomas Weir, Gunner's Mate, Englishman, enlisted at Liverpool.

James Busman, Seaman, Englishman.

Edgar Tripp, Seaman, Englishman, lives in London, enlisted at Liverpool.

John Neil, Seaman, Englishman, lives with his sister in Manchester-street, Liverpool, belongs to Naval Reserve, enlisted at Terceira.

Thomas Winter, Fireman, Englishman, lives in Liverpool; his father is Ticket-collector at the Adelphi Theatre; enlisted at Liverpool.

Samuel Henry, Seaman, Englishman, resides in Liverpool, Naval Reserve Man, enlisted at Liverpool.

John Roberts, Seaman, Welchman, thinks he resides in Liverpool, enlisted at Terceira.

John Duggan, Seaman, Englishman, resides in Liverpool, belongs to Naval Reserve, enlisted at Terceira.

Martin King, Seaman.

Thomas Williams, Seaman, Englishman, resides in Liverpool, belongs to Naval Reserve, enlisted at Terceira.

Robert Williams, Seaman, Englishman, resides in Liverpool, belongs to Naval Reserve, enlisted at Terceira.

Joseph Pearson, Seaman, Englishman, belongs to Chester, enlisted at Liverpool.

Joseph Connor, Seaman, Englishman, resides in Walnut-street ; his wife lives there, and keeps a Butcher's shop ; belongs to Naval Reserve, joined at Terceira.

Thomas McMullen, Seaman, Englishman, resides in Liverpool, joined at Terceira.

Michael Mars, Seaman, Englishman, belongs to Bristol, Naval Reserve, joined at Terceira.

Robert Egan, boy, English, belongs to Chorley.

Malcolm Macfarlane, Seaman, Scotchman, resides in Liverpool, belongs to Naval Reserve, enlisted at Terceira.

Peter Henny, Seaman, Irishman, lives in Liverpool, enlisted at Terceira.

Charles Goodwin, Seaman, Englishman, resides in Liverpool, enlisted at Terceira.

James Hicks, Captain of the Hold, Englishman, enlisted at Liverpool, thinks he resides here.

Robert Parkinson, Wardroom Steward, Englishman, resides in Liverpool, enlisted in Liverpool.

George Appleby, Yeoman, Englishman, resides in Liverpool, married man, enlisted in Liverpool.

John Emory, Seaman, Englishman, resides in Liverpool, belongs to Naval Reserve, enlisted at Terceira.

Wm. Hearn, Seaman, Englishman, resides in Liverpool, belongs to Naval Reserve, enlisted at Terceira,

Thomas L. Parker, Boy, English, stops with Brent Johnson.

A. G. Bartelli, Seaman, Portuguese.

Peter Hughes, Captain of Top, Englishman, resides in Liverpool, belongs to Naval Reserve, enlisted at Liverpool.

Henry Fisher, Seaman, Englishman, resides at Liverpool, enlisted at Liverpool.

Frank Townsend, Seaman, Englishman, enlisted at Liverpool.

George Forrest, Seaman, Irishman, taken off the ship " Manchester " because he had deserted from the " Sumter," and tried by a Court-martial for causing mutiny, and sent on shore in irons to Island Blanco and left there. Previous to his being tried for mutiny he was tied up twenty times in the rigging with his arms spread, for four hours at a time, day and night.

(Signed)   JOHN LATHAM.

Inclosure 3 in No. 26.

Affidavit of Martha Latham.

I, MARTHA LATHAM, of 19, Wellington Street, Swansea, in the county of Glamorgan, wife of John Latham, make oath and say as follows :—

My husband was one of the crew of the steamer " Alabama." In the month of August 1862, my husband, who was in Liverpool, wrote to me that he was going out in the steamer " Bahama " to run the blockade. Some weeks after that I received a letter from my husband dated at the Western Islands, stating that he had joined the steamer " Alabama " for 7l. a-month. On the same day I received another letter from Captain James D. Bullock, inclosing me a half-pay note, signed by Captain Semmes, for the half-pay of my husband while he served on board of said steamer " Alabama." The note was payable to me at Fraser, Trenholm, and Co., in Liverpool. In the latter part of August, or first part of September 1862, my husband's cousin, Thomas Winstanly, 36, Jasper Street, Liverpool, received 5l. for me from the office in Liverpool. I had sent him Captain Bullock's letter, and the one from my husband ; I sent my half-pay note to Liverpool to draw the money on it. It was returned to me in the letter annexed hereto, marked A. I signed my name and sent it to the office of M. G. Klingender and Co , Liverpool, who sent me 3l. 10s., less 7d. the expenses. It was sent me in a Post Office Order, in a letter dated October 3rd, 1862, annexed hereto, and marked on back Exhibit B. On the 31st October, 1862, M. G. Klingender and Co. sent me another letter inclosing me another order for 3*l.* 9*s.* 6*d.*, being another month's half-pay on said note. On the 31st December, 1862, the Messrs. Klingender and Co. sent me another letter inclosing me an order for 3*l.* 9*s.* 6*d.* on account of said half-pay note. The letter is annexed hereto, and marked Exhibit C on the back. I received another half-pay of 3*l.* 9*s.* 6*d.* ; it must have been in January, but the letter in which it was sent, as well as the letter written to me by Captain Bullock above-mentioned, has been mislaid. All the money orders were paid to me. In February or March I received from M. G. Klingender and Co. a letter, without date, stating that my husband had deserted, and stopping the pay on the allotment note. I had been in the habit of sending them the note every time I drew the money ; the last time I sent it they retained it, and sent me the last-mentioned letter, but no money. They still have the allotment note in their possession. The letter from M. G. Klingender and Co., dated 31st of October, 1862, above-mentioned, is annexed hereto, and marked Exhibit D. The last letter from them to me, without date, above-mentioned is also annexed hereto, and marked Exhibit E.

(Signed)   MARTHA LATHAM.

Sworn and subscribed to this 31st day of December, 1863.
   ' (Signed)   J. ROLLY FRIPP, *a Commissioner for taking Oaths in the Court of Queen's Bench at Westminster.*

(A.)
Liverpool, September 30, 1862.

Messrs. M. G. Klingender and Co. must request Mrs. Martha Latham, before paying her the 3*l.* 10*s.*, to sign her name at the back of the allotment note, and then return it to them, when they will remit her a money order for the amount, less cost of order.

Mrs. M. Latham, 19, Wellington Street, Swansea, South Wales.

P.S.—Please note address, No. 22, Water Street, Liverpool.

Exhibit (B).

22, *Water Street, Liverpool, October* 3, 1862.

Mrs. Martha Latham, 19, Wellington Street, Swansea, South Wales.
Madam,
    Inclosed, please find a money order payable at the Post Office of your town for 3*l.* 9*s.* 5*d.* In future you must send us your allotment note signed across a receipt stamp.

Returning you the note, we are, &c.

Per M. G. Klingender & Co.,
(Signed)   C. F. VON MELLE.

	£	s.	d.
Money order	3	9	5
Cost of order	0	0	6
Receipt stamp	0	0	1
	£3	10	0

Exhibit (D).

Liverpool, October 31, 1862.

Mrs. Martha Latham, 19, Wellington Street, Swansea, South Wales.
Madam,
    We inclose you a money order for 3*l.* 9*s.* 6*d.*, payable at the Post-office of your town.

Returning you your note, we are, &c.

Per M. G. Klingender & Co.,
(Signed)   C. F. VON MELLE.

	£	s.	d.
	3	9	6
Cost of order	0	0	6
	£3	10	0

Exhibit (C).

Liverpool, December 31, 1862.

Messrs. Klingender and Co. inclose Mrs. Martha Latham a post-office order for 3*l.* 9*s.* 6*d.*, deducting as usual 6*d.* per cost of order.

No. 19, Wellington Street, Swansea, South Wales.

Exhibit (E).

Martha Latham, 19, Wellington Street, Swansea, South Wales.

Madam,

We have this day received advices per West India mail from St. Domingo, stating that John Latham, with three other men, deserted the "Alabama" on the 25th January, at Kingston, Jamaica, and of course their allotment notes must be stopped.

We are, &c.

Per M. G. Klingender & Co.

(Signed)   C. F. von MELLE.

Inclosure 4 in No. 26.

Affidavit of Thomas Winstinley.

I, THOMAS WINSTINLEY, of Liverpool, in the county of Lancashire, residing at 36, Jasper Street, make oath, and say :—

I am a cousin of John Latham. After he had joined the "Alabama" in the summer of 1862, his wife, Martha Latham, wrote me that Mr. Latham had sent home a part of his advance wages, and requested me to go to Fraser, Trenholm, and Co., in Liverpool, and get it for her.

I went to Fraser, Trenholm, and Co.'s office either the last part of the month of August, or the fore part of September 1862. I saw one of the men in their office. I presented him the note : it was for 5*l.* I forget by whom it was signed. The man said "Well, you are not Martha Latham, and this note is payable to her." I told him she lived at Swansea, and that she had written to me to get it for her, and showed him her letter to me. He then said if I would leave him the letter and note he would pay me. I consented to do this, and he paid me 5*l.*, which I remitted to Martha Latham, less the expenses. The person who paid me I was told by the other clerks in the office was was Fraser, Trenholm, and Co.'s cashier. I left the note and letter with him.

(Signed)   THOMAS WINSTINLEY.

Sworn and subscribed to before me this 6th day of January, 1864, at Liverpool, in the county of Lancaster.

(Signed)   J. PEARSON, *a Commissioner to administer Oaths in Chancery in England.*

No. 27.

Earl Russell to Mr. Adams.

Sir,   *Foreign Office, January* 14, 1864.

I HAVE the honour to acknowledge the receipt of your letter of the 13th instant, inclosing copies of a letter from the Consul for the United States at Liverpool, and of three depositions relative to the case of the "Alabama," and I have the honour to inform you that these papers have been communicated to the proper Department of Her Majesty's Government.

I am, &c.

(Signed)   RUSSELL.

Correspondence respecting the "Alabama."

(In continuation of Correspondence presented to Parliament in March 1863.)

Presented to both Houses of Parliament by Command of Her Majesty. 1864.